Stream Analysis

Stream Analysis

A Powerful Way to Diagnose and Manage Organizational Change

Jerry I. Porras
Stanford University

Addison-Wesley Publishing Company
Reading, Massachusetts • Menlo Park, California • Don Mills, Ontario • Wokingham, England • Amsterdam • Sydney • Singapore • Tokyo • Madrid • Bogotá • Santiago • San Juan

This book is in the Addison-Wesley Series on Organization Development.
Editors: Edgar H. Schein, Richard Beckhard

Other titles in the series:

Organizational Transitions:
Managing Complex Change, Second Edition
Richard Beckhard and Reuben Harris

Organization Development:
A Normative View
W. Warner Burke

Team Building:
Issues and Alternatives, Second Edition
William G. Dyer

The Technology Connection:
Strategy and Change in the Information Age
Marc S. Gerstein

Process Consultation Volume II:
Lessons for Managers and Consultants
Edgar H. Schein

Managing Conflict:
Interpersonal Dialogue and Third-Party Roles,
Second Edition
Richard E. Walton

Library of Congress Cataloging-in-Publication Data

Porras, Jerry I.
  Stream analysis.

  (The Addison-Wesley series on organization development)
  1. Organizational change. I. Title. II. Series.
HD58.8.P67   1987   658.4'06   86–22183
ISBN 0–201–05693–3

Many of the designations used by manufacturers and sellers to distinguish their products are claimed as trademarks. Where those designations appear in this book, and Addison-Wesley was aware of a trademark claim, the designations have been printed in initial caps or all caps.

7 8 9 10 BA 95

To my mother,
Leonela Victoria Porras

Foreword

The Addison-Wesley Series on Organization Development originated in the late 1960s when a number of us recognized that the rapidly growing field of "OD" was not well understood or well defined. We also recognized that there was no one OD philosophy, and hence one could not at that time write a textbook on the theory and practice of OD, but one could make clear what various practitioners were doing under that label. So the original six books by Beckhard, Bennis, Blake and Mouton, Lawrence and Lorsch, Schein, and Walton launched what has since become a continuing enterprise. The essence of this enterprise was to let different authors speak for themselves instead of trying to summarize under one umbrella what was obviously a rapidly growing and highly diverse field.

By 1981 the series included nineteen titles, having added books by Beckhard and Harris, Cohen and Gadon, Davis, Dyer, Galbraith, Hackman and Oldham, Heenan and Perlmutter, Kotter, Lawler, Nadler, Roeber, Schein, and Steele. This proliferation reflected what had happened to the field of OD. It was growing by leaps and bounds, and it was expanding into all kinds of organizational areas and technologies of intervention. By this time many textbooks existed as well that tried to capture the core concepts of the field, but we felt that diversity and innovation were still the more salient aspects of OD today.

The present series is an attempt both to recapture some basics and to honor the growing diversity. So we have begun a series of revisions of some of the original books and have added a set of new authors or old authors with new content. Our hope is to capture the spirit of inquiry and innovation that has always been the hallmark of organization development and to launch with these books a new wave of insights into the forever tricky problem of how to change and improve organizations.

We are grateful that Addison-Wesley has chosen to continue the series and are also grateful to the many reviewers who have helped us and the authors in the preparation of the current series of books.

Cambridge, Massachusetts   Edgar H. Schein
New York, New York   Richard Beckhard

Preface

CHANGE! Over the last three and a half decades, rapid change has been both a plague and an opportunity for organizations. Those who viewed it as something to resist and overcome have atrophied and died. Those who seized it, used it, flowed with it, integrated it, and accelerated it, have, by and large, flourished and prospered.

Warren Bennis, describing the world of organizations as he saw it in 1966, said:

> Everything nailed down is coming loose, . . . no exaggeration, no hyperbole, no outrage can realistically describe the extent and pace of change which modernization involves. In fact, only the exaggerations appear to be true. And it is to our credit that the pseudo horror stories and futuristic fantasies about *increases* in the rate of change fail to deter our compulsive desire to invent, to overthrow, to upset inherited patterns.[1]

Today the rate of change is even greater. Lead by the microelectronics revolution, changes in the demands placed on or-

---

[1] W. G. Bennis, *Changing Organizations* (New York: McGraw-Hill, 1966).

ganizations have been both dizzying and disconcerting. To survive, everyone knows that organizations must change, but the fundamental question facing managers now, as then, is "How?" What must be done to survive in the ever-changing environment? What are the specific things that should be changed? How are they identified? Once identified, how are they changed? What effects do planned changes have on the organization's survival and on the well-being of the organization's employees?

The main purpose of this book is to present Stream Analysis, a powerful new method for providing responses to many of these questions and for guiding planned change in organizations. It is about managing change, the process of diagnosing organizational functioning, planning specific change activities, implementing alterations in a system's character and functioning, and tracking the actions taken. It draws both its intellectual and its applied roots from a wide variety of sources. More than anything, however, it is based on the idea that organizational change can be planned and managed—managed in a more systemic and systematic fashion than it has in the past. Yet, for this to be possible, both managers and change practitioners must have better frameworks for understanding the organizational problems they face and ways of dealing with them. The frameworks should be based on sound fundamental concepts about organizations and people and about the leverage points for organizational change. Altering those leverage points affects individual employees who must, in the end, change the way they behave on the job for systemic change to take place.

The Stream Analysis technique is a broad and general framework. As presented here, some of its analytical dimensions are drawn directly from a theoretical perspective on organizations that I will propose. One attractive side of the stream approach, however, is that the dimensions used in the framework could be different if one held a theory of organization different from mine. In any case, the ax I like to grind is that everyone working in change settings should hold at least *some* theoretical perspective to guide their work. Otherwise, they are operating solely on intuition or on partial views of very complex realities—both shaky foundations for guiding change processes. For Stream Analysis, the reader's theory of organizations could be inserted into the stream framework and used as the basis for its application. The technique is sufficiently robust to handle many views of how organizations function.

Understanding the theoretical underpinnings of any change method or technique is necessary for the method to succeed. Historically, too many planned change efforts have been driven by technique rather than by theory, frequently resulting in the misapplication of whatever technique was being used.[2]

As far back as 1954, Peter Drucker pointed out the absence of theory on how organizations function. He did so while describing the world's movement out of the modern age into what he called an "as yet unnamed era." He noted that as we move into the "post-modern" world we have "no theories, no concepts, no slogans—no real knowledge—about the new reality."[3] Today, we find ourselves in the middle of the same dilemma. On the one hand, the inevitable, rapidly accelerating change in the world forces organizations to respond. On the other hand, we still do not possess a comprehensive set of theories and concepts about what our current states are and how to move into desired future states. We have more knowledge than we did in 1954, but we still lack comprehensive frameworks for understanding the full complexity of organizational dynamics and for guiding the processes of change. This book is an attempt to speak to these needs by providing both a method for guiding the process of change—Stream Analysis—and the basic theoretical framework for understanding organizational dynamics which constitute the underpinnings of this new approach.

Although my main purpose here is to present a technique for improving organization functioning, the reader should have a breadth of knowledge on the dynamics of organizations as background for understanding the technique and why it can be useful for guiding planned change. Based on this, I have argued that anyone trying to change an organization should begin with clear ideas about what an organization is before taking any action.

---

[2]It is important to note that these situations have not always been the fault of those leading the change effort. Instead, they often have reflected the generally thin and incomplete state of planned organizational change theory.

[3]P. F. Drucker, *The Practice of Management* (New York: Harper & Row, 1954).

The book contains two main thrusts. The first is the Stream Analysis method for diagnosing failings in organizational functioning and for planning, implementing, and tracking all needed change actions. The second is the Stream Organization Model, a conceptual basis for Stream Analysis, usable by both managers and change practitioners to understand organizations better and thus what to change in them to improve system functioning.

Chapter 1 begins with several scenarios often encountered in planned change projects and broadly describes how the Stream Analysis approach can help deal with some of the weaknesses in current practice that these scenarios point out. Chapter 2 then describes Stream Analysis in detail, specifying its components and steps for implementation. Chapter 3 begins with a series of fundamental concepts on organizations as systems and on how people learn and change their behavior in them. Based on these concepts, the Stream Organization Model, a framework for understanding organizations from a change perspective is presented next. Chapter 4 presents three examples of the application of Stream Analysis for managing planned change. Chapter 5 offers tips on the effective use of Stream Analysis and discusses some of the traps that exist in its application. The final chapter (Chapter 6) presents an overview and summary, outlining and integrating the Stream Analysis method with the Stream Organization Model.

Since Chapter 3 contains more basic theoretical material, those managers or consultants familiar with much of the organizational change literature may want to skim or skip it and move on to the detailed examples of the application of Stream Analysis. Generally, the technique of Stream Analysis can be understood without a detailed understanding of the theoretical rationale behind it. However, knowing the conceptual underpinnings of any change technique is important for its proper application. So I would urge the less knowledgeable reader to skim Chapter 3 at the very least in order to make sure that the concepts upon which I have based Stream Analysis are familiar and make sense.

As in any project of this nature, there are numerous people who have contributed to it, both intellectually and emotionally.

Like thousands of other authors before me, I would like to thank several of them for all the valuable help they gave me both in the generation of these ideas and in their reactions to earlier versions of this manuscript.

First and foremost, I wish to thank Joan Harkness, manager of the operating room at El Camino Hospital, Mountain View, California. Joan is a wonderful combination of tough-minded manager and expert organization development specialist. Better than anyone I have ever met, she is able to blend skillfully the principles of organization development with the everyday challenges of managing a highly successful organization. Stream Analysis started in her department over six years ago and every day since then she has provided an excellent laboratory for its evolution and development. Without her willingness to use Stream Analysis and innovate with it, many of the ideas presented here would not exist. Coeleen Kiebert was also instrumental in the original conceptualization of Stream Analysis. Working with Joan as a consultant to the operating room department, Coeleen was a central figure in developing Stream Analysis as a research tool. Her background in art strongly influenced the graphic nature of the approach.

Other colleagues, in a loosely connected group we call STREAM, have contributed in a variety of significant ways to the development of this technique. Gary Dexter, working as an external consultant, has applied Stream Analysis in major ways to three organizations. His experiences have contributed greatly to my thinking about the approach and especially to the material presented in the examples chapter and the tips and traps chapter of this book. Emily Lyon, while she was an internal organizational consultant at Lockheed Missiles and Space, was one of the first users of the stream framework and contributed many key ideas to ways in which the technique could be concretely made operational. Susan Hoffer, Tom Robinson, and Peter Robertson, the remaining three members of STREAM, provided numerous ideas during the vast number of discussions the group had about Stream Analysis and how to use it. I would especially like to single out Peter because he has contributed to my intellectual development in many other ways. As a co-author with me on several academic papers, he has helped me to understand organizations better from a theoretical perspective and to sharpen many of the ideas presented here.

Several managers and practitioners have used Stream Analysis and have provided me with material that has in one way or another, influenced me and my thinking about the technique. Doug McCormac, vice president and managing director, TRW Components International; Marge Dunne, former president, Prolog; Vern Glick, director of manufacturing, Lockheed Missiles and Space; Jim Thorne, vice president of human resources, Fisher Controls; Eddie Reynolds, organization development manager, and his group of organizational consultants at Pacific Gas and Electric; Gary Merrill of Drake, Beam, Morin; and, finally, Peter Garne and Dennis McNulty, both organization effectiveness consultants at Lockheed Missiles and Space, are all people I would like to mention and thank.

I would like to express my special appreciation to Milton Johnson, formerly senior editor at Addison-Wesley, for being sufficiently interested in Stream Analysis to include it as part of the OD series. Without his encouragement and support, this book would probably never have been written. Jim Heiter, my current Addison-Wesley editor, deserves special thanks as do Dick Beckhard, Ed Schein, Jim Koch, and Harvey Hornstein, who provided numerous insightful comments on how to improve drafts of the book.

Finally, I wish to thank my wife, Charlene, and my son, Rick, for constantly believing in me and my abilities to accomplish whatever I want. Charlene has made the difference in my life, both personally and professionally, while Rick provides the inspiration to do whatever I can to make the organizations he will inherit better, more effective places in which to work.

Stanford, California   Jerry I. Porras

Contents

1

Introduction

Picture the following scenarios commonly occurring in many planned change efforts:

1. A detailed diagnostic questionnaire was administered to all members of Division Alpha of a large multinational organization. The results were fed back to the top management team who then conducted in-depth analyses of the data. This analytical process led to identifying a set of issues considered to be key problems in the system. When the managers attempted to plan the actions they would take to deal with the problems revealed, they found that they could not reach an agreement on exactly what to do. The source of their difficulties seemed to be that widely diverse interpretations existed about what the data really meant. A typical example concerned the organization's inability to deliver its products according to schedules given customers by the marketing group.

The marketing manager saw the problem as an attitudinal one: If manufacturing really cared about taking care of our customers, they would get the products delivered as promised. A product manager saw it as a scheduling problem: If manufacturing would schedule its activities properly, it would be able to deliver products on time. The engineering manager saw it as a resource problem: If manufacturing had the personnel and machinery to meet the demands placed on it, products would be delivered when promised. The manufacturing manager saw it as a problem of priorities: If marketing wouldn't treat every order as equally important and make unrealistic promises about delivery schedules, we could get the products out on time. As the discussion unfolded, the assumptions held by each manager about what the problem really was never clearly surfaced. Because of all the differing views and the lack of any clear mechanism for revealing the assumptions underlying them, the managers were unable to agree on the best actions to take.

2. A task force representing various areas of the Beta Gas and Electric Company was established to guide a comprehensive planned change process. It made a diagnosis, planned a series of actions, and began implementing them. Broad-scale employee apathy and resistance to the change actions resulted. Upon questioning of several typical organization members, the task force discovered that although numerous memoranda had been sent out announcing and describing the change effort, the average employee felt that he or she knew next to nothing about the changes that were being implemented or the reasons why. Respondents stated that they had filled out a questionnaire and had received a printed summary of the data and some statement about specific actions that were to be taken. They felt that the data summary had been just a bunch of numbers out of which they could make little sense. The actions described made sense but didn't seem to be getting at the problems that were really important; besides respondents didn't understand why the particular actions were chosen in the first place. Finally, they felt they didn't know what was going to happen in the future. As a result, there was much worry and fear about how the changes would affect each person and little motivation to get wholeheartedly involved in the change effort.

3. An extensive planned change process had been going on in the Gamma Microelectronics Company for approximately one year. Frustration about the change effort had been growing over the last four months because problems that had appeared to be

resolved at one point seemed to crop up at a later point. An example mentioned by one frustrated manager related to whom was responsible for making sure that all the data inputs to the monthly product development status report were made in a timely fashion. The manager complained: "I thought we had solved that problem already. Here it is cropping up again. People just aren't coming through with the information as they promised." A second manager pointed out that a similar difficulty existed with the current cost status report: "We agreed that we would handle the product development status report problem by getting people to promise to deliver the information on time. This new problem with the cost report looks pretty similar to the product development report problem and should be handled the same way, but isn't. Why do different versions of the same type of problem keep cropping up?"

4. The manufacturing manager of the Delta Aerospace Corporation was attempting to figure out how to deal with poor relationships between her first level production employees and the quality control staff (a problem revealed by thorough organizational diagnosis). As she studied the situation, she became aware of the fact that any action taken to deal with this problem must also deal with a second, associated but previously unidentified, problem. This second problem was related to the way responsibility for quality was assigned in the plant. Procedures were set up to establish the quality control person as the watch dog, giving the production employees no real responsibility for the quality of the part they produced. The result was constant conflict. The production people did not work carefully because they knew that the quality control people would catch any mistakes. The quality control people were angry at production because they increased the quality control group's workload by depending on them to catch all the errors made.

As this second problem was considered, the manager discovered that there were other interconnected issues that also had to be taken into account. Among these were inconsistencies in performance measurement, ineffectiveness of the reward system in motivating desired behavior, time wasted in production workers going to the quality control facility (located several hundred yards away from the production facility) to discuss deficiencies in parts they produced, and so on. This further probing revealed a larger set of problems all linked together, problems that appeared to be independent of each other in the original diagnosis or problems that were given low priority. The manager became apprehensive, fearing that many of the other problems with high priority for action might have the same character as this one and that perhaps the original diagnosis was woefully incomplete.

5. The Kappa Medical Center, after having been involved in a long-term change effort, decided to conduct a review of the actions taken to date (two years into the project). The analysis revealed much confusion about what had actually been done, the sequence of events, and the reasons behind why the various interventions had been implemented. No means for systematically tracking change activity existed and as a consequence, the change leaders found it difficult to specify what they had learned about how change best took place in their organization. One result was that mistakes in intervention were repeated several times over the course of the change program. An example of an often repeated mistake had to do with the way in which changes in unit responsibilities were introduced to unit members. Most of the departments simply announced to their members what their new responsibilities were. Since departments were each responsible for implementing changes in the responsibilities assigned to each of their units, the consequences of individual approaches were never discussed across departments. The most common result was resistance and hostility to many of the changes implied in the new set of responsibilities. It was not until the two-year review point that the organization realized that prior to any changes in unit responsibilities, they needed to conduct special efforts with each unit both to involve them in the design of their new responsibilities and to help them see the rationale behind the designs suggested by the department managers.

Each of these scenarios describes weaknesses in the approaches typically used to change organizations in a planned way. In the first, the key change leaders did not share a common understanding of the problems identified in the diagnosis. Because the meaning of each problem statement was somewhat different for each person, collectively the group could not agree on the appropriate corrective action. Preferences for different solutions were based on different understandings of the problem's nature.

In the second scenario, apathy and resistance to change were to a large degree the result of lack of understanding and involvement on the part of the typical employee in the organization. The communication effort, although appearing to be sufficient to the change leaders, did not really transmit a sense of what was going on in the change process and why the particular changes were implemented in the first place. Occasional memoranda about the change project failed, in the eyes of most organization members, to inform them sufficiently. With little or no information about the project and its rationale, one response was anxiety with its consequent resistance and apathy.

The third scenario describes what perhaps is the most common failing in planned change activities: the failure to identify the fundamental or core problems of the system. The consequence of this failure entails taking actions that deal with symptoms rather than the more basic problems. The result of implementing solutions to symptoms is that new symptoms keep cropping up again in either identical or similar form. Symptoms resolved do not stay resolved for long but keep coming back, increasing the frustration of all involved in the change activity. Failure to isolate core problems and deal with them generally will lead to failure in the overall change effort.

The fourth scenario describes a situation closely tied to the previous one. In it, problems are viewed as isolated single major issues rather than as interlinked sets of several (if not numerous) other issues. Often these associated issues have been assigned much less importance and have not been selected as targets for immediate action. Yet not attempting to resolve them at the same time as the high-priority problems will lead to ineffective solutions of these latter issues. Attacking a key problem without also attacking, to some degree or another, all of its closely associated problems will, in the end, often not resolve the focal problem.

The fifth and final scenario describes a situation in which relatively little effective organizational learning can take place. Change processes are complicated, with lots of activity going on at the same time. The actions taken, the reasons they are taken, and the actions they trigger are all part of the mosaic of an organization development project. Understanding the ways in which successful change takes place in one's organization is an extremely valuable lesson. In most change efforts, this understanding is never clearly documented or consolidated in ways so that it can be passed on to others or, perhaps more importantly, used to guide future, more effective intervention activity. Learning from the successes and failures of the past is a key way of improving future intervention efforts. If this learning takes place in a haphazard manner, then there is little guarantee that the mistakes of the past might not be repeated. On the other hand, if learning is systematized and readily available, then there is less likelihood that the same mistakes will recur.

Each of these scenarios points to some of the problems frequently encountered when using current techniques for instituting and managing change. In general, today the key failings in planned organizational change efforts revolve around poor or incomplete diagnoses of problems, lack of systematic planning of change interventions, and lack of follow-up to ensure that all the plans that continue to be important to implement are, in fact, implemented.

What the field of organization development needs is a new approach to deal systematically with the current weaknesses in planned change technology. *Stream Analysis* is one potential answer. It is founded on the creation of various types of charts for use in managing the different phases of a planned change process. In the diagnosis phase, it requires users to organize system problems into categories, to place each problem in its proper category on a chart (the Stream Diagnostic Chart), to agree on and show on the diagnostic chart the interconnections that exist among all the problems identified, and then, through an analysis of the resulting chart, to systematically root out the fundamental (or core) problems and the causal chains connecting them to their manifested symptoms.

Once this diagnostic process is completed, Stream Analysis prescribes a planning process based on the Stream Diagnostic Chart called the Stream Planning Chart. Laying out plans in this manner allows users to more easily develop their plans in consonance with the diagnosis and not based on other factors (such as what techniques the change manager or consultant is more familiar or skilled with). Once the implementation of actions is underway, the same charting format can be used to track the change activity. This allows users to document what is happening, to compare actual interventions to both the plans and the problem diagnosis, and to learn how the change process unfolds in their organization.

The Stream approach, therefore, can be used to manage the entire process of change from diagnosis to follow-up. In Stream Charts, change leaders have a mechanism for more effectively understanding underlying organizational dysfunctions, for planning more systematically needed interventions, and for monitoring actual implementation of planned changes.

To understand the power and usefulness of this new approach, let us compare Stream Analysis with some other change theories.

Stream Analysis and Basic Theory

The Stream Analysis approach, like most OD approaches, is rooted in systems theory. It assumes that organizations are open systems; that they consist of various subsystems, each of which can be characterized as consisting of streams of similar variables; that many of these variables are connected, either causally or merely relationally, to other variables both within their same stream or across streams; and that instituting actions which change one variable will be resisted by other connected variables which are not targets of intervention. At the same time, these other connected variables will be affected by changes in the original variable.

Stream Analysis supplements systems theory by graphically representing the complex set of relationships that exist in an organizational problem situation. Systems theory proposes wide numbers of interconnections among subsystems and with this, numerous interconnections among problems across the same subsystems. The main deficiency in systems theory as applied to organizations is that great difficulty arises in making sense of all the interrelationships it proposes. With the Stream Analysis approach, the numerous interrelationships are charted and can be visually analyzed by tracking through the charts and identifying sets of connected problems. These problem sets can then be extracted from the charts and analyzed separately, a process that yields much greater understanding of the issues and how they are connected and what actions must be taken to deal with them both individually and as a complex of interconnected problems.

Stream Analysis is also rooted in social cognitive theory,[1] a perspective describing the mechanisms through which people learn new behaviors. Social cognitive theory emphasizes the effects of environment on the behavior of people in it. People are influenced by the messages they receive from the settings they are in, messages that affect their expectations both about their own abilities and about what they will get out of behaving in the manner signaled by their environment. Stream Analysis operationalizes these ideas by mapping out the complex set of organizational factors in which people work. Through an analysis of the problems existing in each of these arenas, it is possible to understand why people are behaving in dysfunctional ways. Furthermore, the pattern of new environmental conditions that must be created to change employee behavior can also be mapped using techniques of Stream Analysis.

In summary, systems theory and social cognitive theory provide the conceptual foundations for Stream Analysis. The technique supplements these basic theories by supplying a means for operationalizing the abstract concepts contained in each of them. It therefore extends them both and makes them more relevant to everyday organizational life.

Stream Analysis and OD Theory

A recent review of OD theory presented a framework for organizing the broad array of theories in the field.[2] The essence

[1]A. Bandura, *Social Foundations of Thought and Action: A Social Cognitive Theory* (Englewood Cliffs, N.J.: Prentice-Hall, 1986).

[2]J. Porras and P. J. Robertson, Organization development theory: a typology and evaluation. In R. W. Woodman and W. A. Pasmore (eds.), *Research in Organization Development*, vol. 1 (Greenwich, Conn.: JAI, 1987).

of that framework was a division of OD theory into two broad classes: 1) implementation theory (theory that focuses on activities change agents must undertake in effecting planned change) and 2) change process theory (theory that describes the dynamics through which organizational variables change as a consequence of intervention). Implementation theory was then subdivided into a) strategy theories (theories that focus on the strategies used to change a system), b) procedure theories (theories that outline the specific steps and procedures needed to change a system), and c) technique theories (theories that describe one particular technique for intervening on a limited set of organizational variables).

Broadly speaking, Stream Analysis is a procedure theory. It is an implementation theory that outlines the particular steps and procedures needed to carry out a change process. It draws its basic components from the action research model, as do most procedure theories, and specifies a set of key variables for both diagnosis and change.[3] However, unlike other theories of this type, Stream Analysis is graphics-based. This technique makes it possible to chart out the problems identified in the key variables specified by the approach. Interestingly, this is an area in which Stream Analysis can uniquely complement any of the other procedure theories of OD. The charting technique is not bound by the particular variable set specified by Stream Analysis. Indeed, any set of variables seen as central to a particular theoretical perspective can be inserted into the Stream Charts and used as the basis for an organizational diagnosis.

This makes it possible for change leaders, operating in a wide variety of settings or basing their intervention activity on a diverse set of theories (and thus a diverse set of organizational

---

[3]Some typical examples of procedure theories are those proposed in the following publications: E. F. Huse and T. G. Cummings, *Organization Development and Change*, 3rd ed. (St. Paul, Minn.: West, 1985); W. L. French and C. H. Bell, *Organization Development: Behavioral Science Interventions for Organization Improvement*, 3rd ed. (Englewood Cliffs, N.J.: Prentice-Hall, 1984); N. M. Tichy, *Managing Strategic Change: Technical, Political, and Cultural Dynamics* (New York: John Wiley and Sons, 1983); W. W. Burke, *Organization Development* (Boston: Little, Brown, 1982); D. A. Nadler, Managing organizational change: an integrative perspective. *Journal of Applied Behavioral Science 17* (1981):191–211; M. Beer, *Organization Change and Development* (Santa Monica, Calif.: Goodyear, 1980).

variables targeted for diagnosis and change), to use the Stream Analysis framework. It is not bound to one type of organizational setting or to any one theoretical perspective. This, then, is a very important gap in current OD technology filled by the Stream approach. It provides a tool for implementing change more effectively by diagnosing, planning, and tracking the actions implemented.

Conclusion

As a new technique for diagnosing, planning, and tracking organizational change, Stream Analysis contains several important characteristics that uniquely contribute to the process of managing planned change. First, it is graphics-based. Its visual nature is central to its effectiveness because when people see visual representations of complex phenomena, they tend to understand the phenomena better as well as remember longer what they have understood. It helps them to keep from getting confused as they are inundated with more and more data. Those readers who have worked on planned change know that one thing typical of most OD efforts is the generation of reams of data. The challenge is always how to make sense out of all the information that accrues. In my experience, being able to pictorially represent organizational issues and the relationships among them has always been an effective way to achieve an understanding of what is going wrong, the first major step in any intervention process.

A second attribute of the Stream Analysis approach is that it can be used in several key stages of intervention — in finding out what is going wrong, in planning what to do about it, and in keeping track of what was done. Thus, it can help make the process more comprehensible to all organization members, not just those leading the change activity. So, it is a potent communication device, useful in letting people know what is going on. I have found that much resistance to change occurs because people do not know what is happening or what might be happening in the future. The charts generated by this approach can serve this purpose well. In so doing, they can also provide a mechanism for getting broader input into the change process. Using the Stream

Charts as the vehicle, every member of an organization can better understand the change activity and provide feedback about it to those responsible for managing the intervention process.

Stream Analysis is also quite flexible and can be adapted to a wide variety of contexts or theoretical perspectives (even though it was derived out of one particular set of concepts). Users can determine the organizational variables they see as most central and insert them into the charting process which is the basis of the approach. Resulting diagnoses and action plans will then reflect the organizational areas and change leverage points deemed most relevant by the leaders of the specific change activity.

Finally, in any change process, Stream Analysis can be used either extensively or only in limited ways. Two dimensions might be relevant in deciding the extent to which the technique would be used:

- Who would use it?
- Through which stages of a change project might it be used?

In the first arena, Stream Analysis could be done by a manager alone or by a consultant wanting to have a clearer idea of each stage of change. It could be done by a small change management team, responsible for guiding the intervention effort, or larger numbers of organization members could participate more extensively in various steps of the analysis. The scope of involvement in the use of the technique would need to be guided by the intentions and assumptions of those leading the change, but the technique is sufficiently flexible to be used effectively by different types of organization groups.

In the second arena, the technique could be used only in the diagnostic phase, in both the diagnostic and planning phase, or in the diagnostic, planning, and implementation phases. Furthermore, it could be used in any one phase without needing to be used in either of the other two. It has the capability of assisting in the managing of each phase without needing to be connected to the remaining ones. This is not to say that there wouldn't be distinct advantages to using it across all three phases. Rather, there is some level of independence in the way it is used in each of these three stages of any planned change activity.

With this broad perspective on Stream Analysis, we can now turn to a more detailed description of the technique. The next chapter presents the basic components of the approach along with some brief examples in which to ground the ideas organizationally.

2

Foundations of Stream Analysis

Complexity in the way organizations go about getting their work done makes it extremely difficult to figure out precisely where organizational problems arise. Malfunctions in organizational operations typically manifest themselves in the form of some output not meeting a desired standard. For example, customer complaints might multiply to an unacceptable level, quality may drop below standard, absenteeism or turnover may increase, costs may rise, or sales may decrease. These would all be indications that the organization is not functioning effectively, but they would only be the tip of the iceberg. Underneath all these output difficulties are the more fundamental roots of those problems seen above the surface. These submerged problems also exist in layers, with the ones nearer the surface symptomatic of the basic problems deeper down.

The main challenge to anyone trying to improve an organization's functioning is to identify correctly the core problems causing ineffective functioning. Yet, with the several layers of other, less fundamental problems obscuring the truly core issues the system needs to change, organizations wind up attacking problems that are symptoms and find that the problems keep popping back up, often in slightly different forms. This generally leads to much frustration and disillusionment about the change process and whether or not the whole effort is worth it.

A roadmap, which can guide the diagnosis of organizational ills, is essential for tracking down the core issues and setting the stage for more effective change activity. Stream Analysis can provide just such a roadmap.

Stream Analysis is a mechanism for mastering problems that block effective organizational functioning. Using it entails ferreting out the issues at the root of the difficulties facing a system. Once problems are identified, Stream Analysis also provides an approach, consistent with the diagnostic procedure, to planning change activity. Finally, as change is implemented, the Stream Analysis technique can be used to monitor intervention activity by tracking the specific change actions taken, their sequence, and the relationships among them.

With these points as a background, let us now turn to a detailed description of this approach, focusing first on its rationale, then turning to its use as a diagnostic tool, as a planning approach, and as a device for tracking and learning how change takes place in the target organization.

Stream Analysis Concepts

The Stream Analysis approach is based on creating graphic representations of the three central components of any planned organizational change process: 1) problem diagnosis, 2) planning, and 3) intervention.

Problem Diagnosis

In organizations, problems exist over time. They ebb and flow. Some survive for long periods while others crop up, then quickly disappear. Some problems eventually take care of themselves while others seem intractable and somehow never appear to get solved. Much of an organization's life is spent identifying problems and dealing with them so that the productive work of the organization can get done. For managers, a good portion of the workday is spent solving problems that get in the way of effective organizational functioning.

The Stream approach to system diagnosis is based on pictorially representing these organizational problems on a chart. The chart, called a Stream Diagnostic Chart, is divided into columns (streams), one for each organizational dimension considered key by the user of the chart.[1] Each problem, after having been identified, is categorized as primarily reflecting difficulties in one stream and a brief description of it is placed in the appropriate column.

The next step in Stream Analysis is to specify the key interconnections that exist among the categorized problems. Analysis of these interconnections results in arrows drawn on the chart to represent all the relationships identified. A somewhat simplified version of a final Stream Chart might look like the one shown in Fig. 2–1. It will yield insights into patterns of problems as well as their centrality — that is, whether they are symptomatic or core problems.

Planning Interventions

Planning of the intervention activities can be accomplished with a chart similar to the one used for diagnosis except that, in this case, the vertical axis of the Stream Chart now represents time (See Fig. 2–2). Users familiar with Program Evaluation and Review Technique (PERT) charts will recognize many similarities between this planning approach and that one. A main difference is that the Stream Analysis technique requires that actions taken to intervene into the organization be placed in a column representing the organizational dimension most affected by the intervention.

Tracking the Change Process. The final part of the Stream approach is the Stream Tracking Chart. This chart looks exactly like the Planning Chart shown in Fig. 2–2 except that it contains information describing what actually happened rather than what was planned.

---

[1]The description assumes that four key dimensions have been identified. For ease in presentation, these four dimensions are labeled 1) Organizing Arrangements, 2) Social Factors, 3) Technology, and 4) Physical Setting. These labels have not been selected at random but rather, relate to the theoretical perspective presented in the next chapter.

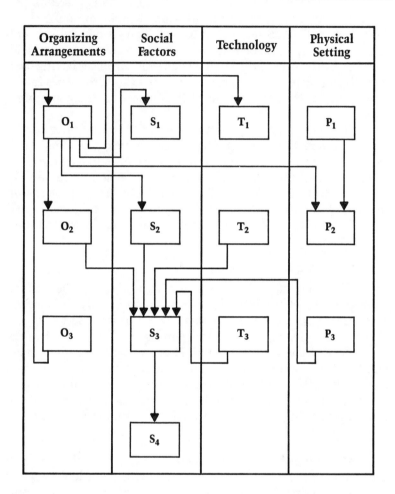

Figure 2–1
Stream Diagnostic Chart

With this brief overview in mind, let us now turn to a more detailed description of the three phases of Stream Analysis and how the process of planned change is guided using this framework.

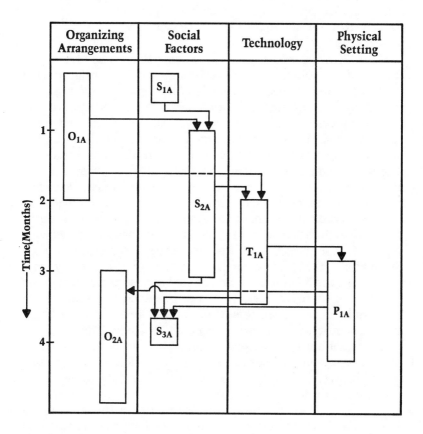

Figure 2–2
Stream Planning/Tracking Chart

Stream Analysis Procedures

The actual procedures through which a Stream Analysis is performed will be described in the following sections with a few brief examples embedded in the discussion. For the present purposes, we will focus on the mechanics of the technique so as to keep the description as clear as possible. In a subsequent chapter, three detailed cases will be presented to provide the richness needed to better understand this approach.

1. Forming a Change Management Team. The first step in the use of the Stream Analysis technique is quite similar to what is done in most change approaches: the formation of a cross-sectional group of organizational members to guide and monitor the change process. This group, known as the *change management team* (CMT) works best when it represents all of the important segments and levels participating in the change process. Key in this step is to include some people with extreme points of view, for it is these perspectives that often need to be examined more fully in complex environments. They can yield critical insights into the true nature of an organization's problems, insights often missed by those holding somewhat more homogeneous views.[2] If it is not practical for such a team to be formed, then the next best thing is to create a group consisting of the key managers in the organization. These should be those people who must support the change process if it is to be effective. Should it not be feasible to form even this level of team, then the responsible manager must lead the change process all alone. The latter situation is not optimal, since widespread support of the change activities is needed to ensure success. It *is* possible to execute successful change with only the manager leading the process, but it is just more difficult to pull off.

The discussion below will assume that a change management team has been formed to guide the change activity. It will be referred to as CMT and can describe the actions taken by a group or solely by the manager if a full team was not formed.

2. Collecting Data. To deal productively with the broad set of issues blocking a system's effective performance, it is necessary to "take a snapshot" of those issues and try to freeze them at a point in time. This snapshot distorts reality a bit because the organization never stands still, and neither do its problems. How-

---

[2]Ralph Kilman's book *Beyond the Quick Fix* proposes this perspective. It should be consulted for additional elaboration of this point.

ever, by necessity, we must assume that the snapshot of the organization's problem set taken at one point in time is not dramatically different from the reality that would exist at a second point, the time when one would be taking the actions needed to solve previously identified problems. Clearly, the gap between time 1 and time 2 should not be too large or the real situation when actions are taken may wind up being too different from the situation that existed at the time of the diagnosis.

This snapshot of the organization, the first step in the diagnostic process, begins with the gathering of information about how the organization is malfunctioning as it tries to accomplish its purpose. A variety of sources may be consulted for information on the organization's problems. Optimally, all organizational members should be asked for their opinion, but this is not always possible, especially in large organizations. Typically, a sample of people drawn from different areas and levels in the organization is used as the source of information for a diagnosis.

The consultant or change agent can gather the needed information in a variety of ways:

1. Interview people who could present useful insights into what is going wrong
2. Circulate a written questionnaire designed to pick up a wide range of problems
3. Observe organization members at work or the conditions of the work setting
4. Analyze various company records

Interviews require considerable resources and, if the number of respondents is large, it is virtually impossible to gather data in a timely fashion using this approach. In addition, once gathered, there can be great difficulty in handling all the data generated by this method. If interviews are taped, it is a laborious task either to listen to all the interviews and code what was said or to transcribe them first and then code the resulting hard copy. In either case, the process is both time consuming and expensive.

My colleagues and I have experimented with variations of the traditional interview in an attempt at generating the richness of information produced by this technique while at the same time avoiding the pitfalls inherent in it.[3] In one organization, all the employees were divided into small groups of approximately fifteen people. Each group was asked to do some preliminary work before meeting to share their views of the organization's functioning. Their assignment was to list all the problems they saw in the organization — what blocked them from doing their jobs better; what blocked others from doing their jobs better; what kept the organization from performing at a higher level of effectiveness; and so on.

When the group met, a leader was appointed and given responsibility for writing all the information provided by the group members on flip chart sheets. The leader was also responsible for making sure that a positive brainstorming atmosphere existed, that there be no evaluation of the perceptions presented by the group members. The goal was to get out as much honest data as possible.

With this as a starting point, the procedure consisted of participants describing in turn one problem they saw in the organization's functioning. Once an individual had presented an issue, the next person would have a turn at presenting an issue, then the next, and so on. When all participants had had the opportunity to present something, the cycle would be repeated with the first person describing another problem, and so on. Anyone who did not have a new problem to offer would pass and wait for another turn. If by that time the person had thought of something new, he or she could present it then. The group would continue going around the room soliciting problem descriptions from its members until everyone passed. At that point it was assumed that all problems of which people were aware had been mentioned and the data-gathering phase would end.

A second method for more efficiently gathering data through face-to-face interviews focused on the way the information received was recorded. In this technique, the person conducting the interview wrote the information provided by the respondent on a form that had been set up like a Stream Chart.[4] Whenever the person being interviewed described a problem, the

---

[3]This technique was suggested to us by Doug McCormac.
[4]This approach was first developed by Emily Lyon.

interviewer would write it in the appropriate stream column. At the end of the interview, the interviewer would quickly scan the data sheets and be prompted to ask further questions about streams that appeared to be underrepresented with information. This ensured that information was collected about potential problems in all streams, and not just the most obvious ones. It is important to note that this technique tends to undermine the process of problem assignment to streams by the CMT. This process, as will be discussed later, is important in achieving the shared understanding of problems that is so important for coordinated intervention.

Questionnaires can reach large numbers of people but are limited in the type of information that can be collected. They must be structured clearly, which means that the creator of the questionnaire needs to have a fairly clear idea of the issues at work in the organization before creating the questionnaire. One approach to defining a questionnaire is to use the stream dimensions as a guide, and create a set of questions that will focus on each of the subcategories of each stream. An advantage to doing this is that the same questionnaire, with minor modifications, could be used across all parts of a large organization and would serve to build up a set of baseline data. These data could be used later as a source of comparison for information collected from any particular segment of the organization. If those parts of the organization performing particularly well are characterized by certain unique profiles of questionnaire data, then those profiles could help other, lower performing groups better interpret what their data might mean for them. In any case, having the data organized by streams makes it easy to make the transition from the problem categorization phase of Stream Analysis to the problem interconnection step.

Observing people on the job is a third way of collecting information on organizational problems, albeit a costly and time consuming one. A substantial amount of time must be spent before data collection in order to create appropriate relationships with organization members. They would need to trust the individual gathering information before they would behave normally while being observed. Once trust has been established, this approach yields very rich data about what people are actually doing, not what they say they are doing. From this perspective, the quality of information can be much higher using an observation-based technique for data collection.

Company records contain information about the performance of the company, turnover, absenteeism, grievances, minutes of meetings, records of key decisions, and more. They are mainly useful for gathering output data or information that can give a historical perspective on the organization. Company records often provide the only source of hard data about the functioning of the organization and, as such, are quite useful as reinforcers of the conclusions drawn from data collected through "softer" means.

Generally, the information needed for a diagnosis is obtained using a combination of techniques rather than just one. The specific methods used to gather information are determined by the number of people to be surveyed and the resources available to the organization for a data collection process. In any case, the output of this data gathering process would be statements of the problems affecting the performance of the organization.

3. Categorizing Problems. Once problem statements are generated, they are then presented to the CMT for discussion and categorization into one of the organizational dimensions. The dimensions are called *streams* to denote that they consist of either issues or actions flowing over time. The CMT is responsible for placing each problem into one of the streams and, in order to do this, must have discussed the problem in sufficient depth such that a shared understanding of it is achieved by all the team members.

This shared understanding is a key step in the diagnostic process. Since in most problem situations people's views of problems depend on where they sit, providing a mechanism that forces in-depth discussion is of fundamental importance. The CMT must work out its own method for ultimately deciding the stream in which each problem will be placed. The only requirement is that sufficient discussion occur so that everyone understands the problems in the same way. From this perspective, it is not of central importance that any problem be categorized in any particular stream. In fact, for some problems, there might not be a "correct" stream. In these cases, there is no right or wrong categorization. Once again, it is the shared understanding that is the end to be achieved.

As the problems are categorized, they are placed on Stream Charts in their appropriate columns. After all identified problems have been classified, an analysis of the entire set usually reveals much overlap among the various problem statements. What is usually required then is a grouping of problems and a condensation of the larger set of problems into a much smaller collection of relatively unique issues.

4. Identifying Interconnections. The next step is to identify interconnections that exist among the problems charted. Here the issues are several:

1. Does one problem seem to be driving or causing the other?
2. Is one problem simply related to another with no evident causal relationship?
3. Is one problem seeming to cause as well as be caused by another?
4. Is there no clear and reasonably significant relationship between one problem and any other?

Items 2 and 3 should be avoided in determining interconnections. Every effort should be made to establish a direction of causality once a relationship is identified as existing. Later analyses will be unnecessarily complicated by having "two-headed" arrows. For this reason, a decision on direction should be forced even though the CMT might feel ambivalent.

Since there often are a reasonably large number of problems identified in the earlier stages of this analysis, care must be taken to avoid overloading the process by specifying relatively unimportant interconnections. Question 4, therefore, is an important one to keep in mind when managing the complexity of this step in the procedure.

Once again, an important factor in this process is the shared understanding that can be achieved when the CMT comes to an agreement about the linkages among the set of problems identified as key blocks to organizational effectiveness. Discussions of "what causes what" bring to light a wide range of opposing views of the world which often have been the source of disagreement in the past. Furthermore, it is mainly through an agreement on causes of problems that agreement on solutions can take place. Many change activities have failed because the people implementing solutions have disagreed over the nature of the problems they were trying to alleviate.

A completed diagnostic chart might look like the one shown earlier in Fig. 2–1. Analysis of this chart begins to reveal the information needed for a thorough diagnosis of the situation. We will point out some of its interesting characteristics and explain what they might imply.

5. Analyzing the Problem Chart. Symptoms (problems caused by deeper problems) are highly visible in the organization and often driven by a relatively large number of other problems. If one were to spend five minutes in an organization, many of the organization's symptoms would be mentioned numerous times by members of the organization. Just such a problem type is represented by S_3 in the Stream Chart. It has several arrows going into it signifying that numerous other problems are driving it. As such, we would call it a symptom. Taking care of symptoms will not do much to eliminate problems that drive them and, as a consequence, they could be expected to return either in the same form or in some altered shape — but they would return, nevertheless.

A second type of problem reflected in the chart is one like O_1. This problem has many arrows coming out of it signifying that it is driving many of the other problems in the organization. O_1 is a core problem and solving it would do much to reduce the existence of all the problems it drives. A tremendous amount of leverage can be gained by resolving problems like O_1.

A third type of problem is represented by O_3. This problem is sitting there all by itself, not connected to much else except O_1. Since it is driving a problem that is itself driving numerous other problems, rectifying it will have even more leverage than solving O_1 directly. This type of problem, one that drives core problems, is a *fundamental core* problem. They often do not exist or cannot be easily identified, but, when they can, they provide maximum "bang for the buck" when taken care of.

Often, the most interesting observations made possible by organizing the data in this manner relate to problem stories that run through the data. A story is a collection of problems strung together that, when taken as a group, describe a more complex problem in the organization. Stories show up in the Stream Charts as more or less vertical clusters of interlinked problems. An example of what this might look like is shown in Fig. 2–3. (This figure only shows the linkages that contribute to the problem story with the problems constituting the story enclosed by the thick black line.)

The two core problems O_1 and P_1 drive a cluster of connected problems that eventually lead to the symptom S_6. There is a logic to the pattern of problems that can be explained in storylike fashion.

One example of a problem story starts with a prevalent symptom, many unresolved interpersonal conflicts. Tracing back through a problem chart might reveal the following story that explains why the conflict situation exists. A core problem, that the goals of the organizational unit have not been clearly established (O_1), leads to a lack of clarity about who is responsible for which decisions (O_2). This ambiguity results in the wrong people making particular decisions (S_2), which means that many of the decisions made seem also to be wrong (S_5). One consequence of this situation is that people wind up blaming others for the poor decisions that are made, which then leads to much unresolved interpersonal conflict (S_6).

The second part of the story starts out with a problem in the physical setting. The physical environment in the manufacturing plant is dusty (P_1), which contributes to the breakdown of key equipment (T_2). These breakdowns highlight the fact that the technicians assigned to operate the equipment are not technically skilled to repair it (T_3). Because of their lack of skill, they are unable to respond to the pressures placed on them by their supervisors and wind up feeling severely stressed (S_4). In their highly stressed condition, they are short-tempered and become involved in a lot of conflict with both co-workers and supervisors (S_6).

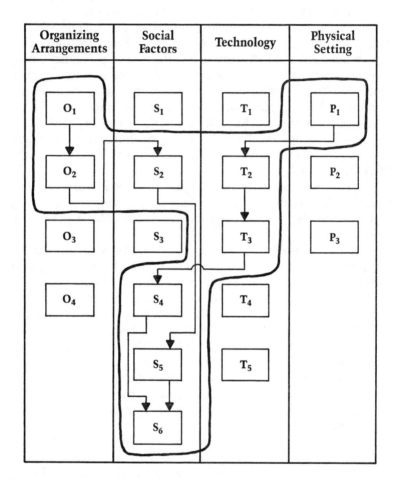

Figure 2–3
Stream Diagnostic Chart — Story Example

Another type of pattern that often shows up in a Stream Chart consists of a theme of core problems. Themes are sets of core problems that are more or less horizontally distributed in the chart and which, although they are not formally interlinked, all speak to some common issue. An example of what this might look like on a Stream Chart is shown in Fig. 2–4. The theme is enclosed by the thick black line.

In this case, one theme would consist of core problems O_2, S_2, T_1, and P_1. These more macro problems should be identified because they require integrated actions for solution.

An example of a core problem theme might be a "firefighting mentality" in the organization. This theme could consist of problems such as the following: 1) The structure of the organization is overloaded with expediter roles while, at the same time, the planning function is understaffed (O_2). 2) People are admired only if they come through in a crisis and not respected if they do their jobs in a timely fashion (S_2). 3) The machinery in the manufacturing plant is mainly set up for crash jobs and not enough of it is designed to produce large quantities of product at low cost, which is what a large segment of what the firm's market demands (T_1). 4) The open office design makes it extremely difficult to have any quiet, uninterrupted time for planning (P_1). All of these problems can be thought of as part of a more global problem and, as a package, each provides one component of the overall firefighter issue. Solving a problem like this would require attacking it across the many fronts in which it manifests itself.

6. Formulating a Plan of Action. Once the diagnosis has been completed, the next step in the Stream Analysis approach is to create an action plan consistent with the identified problems. The action plan is laid out in much the same format as the diagnostic chart with the exception that the vertical axis now reflects a time dimension.

The actions to be taken are placed in columns corresponding to the organizational dimension they most strongly affect. Certain types of change interventions affect more than one organizational stream. In this case, the action should be placed in the stream it most affects and, probably more important, in the stream containing the problem targeted for change by the intervention.

It is very important to note that planning too far into the future is unrealistic, and perhaps even counterproductive. Plans of three to nine months are probably the most appropriate. Be-

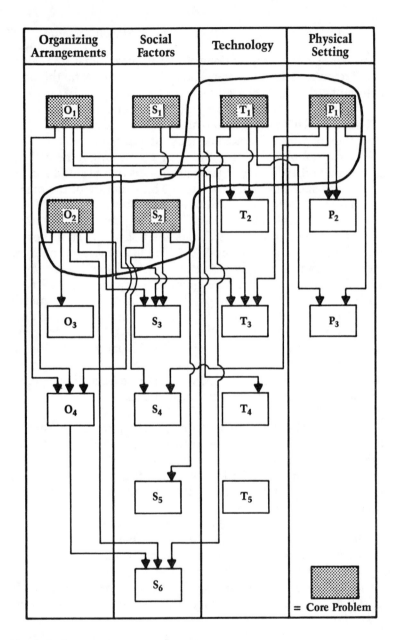

Figure 2–4
Stream Diagnostic Chart — Theme Example

yond that, things start to get pretty tenuous and it is unrealistic to expect to live up to the plans that stretch out much farther than that.

The main advantage of laying out an action plan in the same format as a problem diagnosis is that it can help keep clear the rationale for the various actions being taken. Complex change processes create great confusion as to why certain things are being done and why other things are not. With a chart that can show a clearer mapping from problems to actions, this type of confusion can be reduced, although never completely eliminated. Another side of this is that managers often have "pet solutions" that they try to use whenever anything goes wrong. They will often interpret problems in the context of the solutions they have at their disposal. In a sense they are like the person with a hammer who sees everything as a nail.

Having the actions laid out in such a fashion that they can be easily mapped into the problems they are intended to solve makes it more difficult for managers who suffer from the pet solution syndrome to take inappropriate actions. They are forced to face the problems more directly and ask themselves does this action really deal with the problems that have been identified.

7. *Tracking the Intervention Process.* As change actions are implemented, the final use of the Stream Analysis approach comes into play. Interventions can be tracked on a chart whose format is similar to that of the planning chart. The only difference is that the content of the boxes describes what actually happened rather than what was planned to happen. All the unanticipated actions that were taken are charted, thus giving the organization a clear picture of exactly what transpired.

There are several advantages to maintaining a record of actions taken, the most important of which is that the tracking document provides a mechanism through which an organization can better learn how to change itself. By analyzing what it did, those who are most responsible for leading the change process can begin to understand what works and what does not and from this, be more effective in planning future change activities.

An important example of how this learning can take place occurred in one organization that had been involved in a planned change process for several years. They had not been using the Stream Analysis as a guide, but the manager of the group had been keeping thorough records of the activities in which the group had engaged. It was at this stage that the manager learned about Stream Analysis and decided to lay out all of the previous change activity in the tracking chart format. This seemed like a good way to learn more about the technique while at the same time test it out and see if it could be helpful.

The first two years of the planned change process were charted and revealed a situation that demonstrates how organizations can learn about change from an analysis of a tracking chart. It seemed that this organization had created a series of highly specialized, but also highly interdependent, work teams, each led by a manager. These team managers were also part of a management group that dealt with the interdependent problems that were part of how the new organizational form was intended to operate.

The tracking chart showed that the new organizational structure (Organizing Arrangements stream) had been put into place in month 3 of the project. It also showed that in month 9, a sequence of team-building activities (Social Factors stream) were instituted with the management team described above. When queried about the need for and timing of the team building, the manager remarked that the "situation had gotten so bad we had to do something to get that team to work together. All the management team members had been in the same department with one another for several years so we didn't expect that they would have so much trouble getting things done when they were put together as part of an interdependent team."

The organization's members learned that they had restructured their organization and had created an interdependent team that needed some developmental work to help it to function effectively. They did not do the needed team building until the situation was so desperate that they were essentially forced to do something drastic. In effect, there was a *hole* in the intervention process: no intervention occurred where one was needed.

It is important to note that the organization had not learned from having to do the team building six months later that they had made a mistake by not doing it immediately after the restructuring. It was not until they saw the tracking chart and began to analyze why they did what they did, that they realized their error and vowed never to repeat it. I tracked their change process for another six years and they never made that mistake again.

A second important use of the tracking charts relates to how and what information about the change process is communicated to organization members participating in it. Often, in any complex and long-term change effort, people in the organization, especially those at the bottom of it, begin to lose sight of what is going on and why. Managers, and others more closely involved with the change planning and intervention, fail to communicate regularly with subordinates to let them know what is happening.

A typical consequence of this situation is that people become disillusioned or cynical about the change effort. They claim, and rightly so, that there was a lot of hoopla and activity when the process began. During the diagnosis phase, they were being interviewed and asked for their opinions. They were involved in helping generate a greater understanding of the problems facing the organization and knew much about the effort in general. After some months, when the planning was finished and some visible changes were put in place, then it seemed like nothing else was happening. It is during these periods that it is critical for people to know that things are still happening and that the process is moving forward. Without their support and involvement, any change process is sure to slow down and eventually wither away.

I have found that the tracking charts provide an excellent method of dealing with this problem and effectively communicating what is going on. Making them visible to people in the organization on a regular basis allows everyone to understand that things are happening, exactly the actions being taken, and when.

In fact, the three sets of charts, the diagnostic, planning, and tracking charts, can all serve the purpose of communicating the change process to the entire organization. In one organization, the Stream Charts were placed on the walls of the main employee lounge. Initially, the Stream Diagnostic Charts were put up with large blank sheets of paper taped right next to them. The blank paper served as a graffitti space for employees to feed back comments about the problems they saw defined in the charts. If they thought that things were missing from the diagnosis, they would say so on the blank sheets. After a few days, the information from the graffitti sheets was analyzed and relevant new additions were made to the diagnostic chart.

Once the diagnosis was considered complete, plans were developed and the Stream Planning Charts were also placed on the walls for all to see. In this way, everyone in the organization could see which problems were being attacked, what specific actions were planned, and the timing of each anticipated change activity. The same procedure for reacting to the diagnosis was used to generate feedback on the plans established.

When the change plan began to be implemented, the Stream Tracking Charts were also placed on the walls next to the other two sets. As new activities would be undertaken, the tracking charts would be updated, making it possible for everyone to be kept current on the progress of the entire effort.

Every employee, as he or she walked into the lounge area, could see all three sets of Stream Charts, would know what was happening and, because each chart was visible and could be compared with every other chart, had an understanding of exactly what was going on and why certain interventions were taking place. Much of the resistance that normally takes place in any change process may have been reduced because people knew what was going on, felt that they had an input to help shape the process, and were considered important enough that the organization would take the time and effort to keep them informed and involved in a meaningful way.

Key Assumptions

Before closing this chapter, it would be very useful to discuss a few key assumptions of Stream Analysis, especially in relation to the role of a consultant in the process. Stream Analysis can and has been conducted without the help of a skilled professional consultant. It has worked and worked reasonably well. This is not to say that it does not work better with consultant help, because it does. Consultants contribute in at least two important ways. First, they can provide the skilled group facilitation that is often needed to help the CMT function more effectively. Development of the problem chart can be especially tumultuous, with much conflict, miscommunication, and frustration. A good process facilitator would substantially improve the quality of problem identification and analysis. Second, the consultant can provide much "expert" insight into the issues identified, into their interrelationships, and into their deeper meanings and implications. Using his or her experience as a basis, the consultant can dramatically improve the quality of analysis by asking probing questions, providing information, making interpretations, and bringing a theoretical base into the discussion.

So, although consultants can play very useful roles in the Stream Analysis process, it can be effectively conducted without them. It is important to note that if a consultant is involved, the managers and the CMT must still take responsiblity for leading the change process and not feel as if they can pass it off to the outside professional.

A second assumption implicit in this approach deserves further discussion also. We assume that the CMT, using a group consensus process, will produce an effective diagnosis when aided by Stream Analysis. Certainly, this will not happen if disagreements or extreme perspectives are suppressed in the drive toward consensus. The resistor or extremist can play a key role in developing an accurate diagnosis. For this reason, individuals taking dissenting positions must be nurtured and listened to. However, at some point, consensus must be reached or else the diagnosis cannot proceed. The art of using Stream Analysis involves being able to manage the process of supporting differing points of view while at the same time moving toward a consensually derived diagnosis of the situation.[5]

Conclusion

The Stream Analysis approach can be used for diagnosing organizational problems, planning change activities, and tracking

---

[5]This is clearly an area in which an outside consultant can be of great help in facilitating the process of consensus while at the same time facilitating the expression of differing points of view.

the intervention process that unfolds. Briefly, the steps in the approach are

1. Put together a change management team (CMT).
2. Collect information about the malfunctionings of the organization and make a list of all the problems identified.
3. Present this information to the CMT, and have the team consensually assign each problem into one stream and place it on a Stream Diagnostic Chart.
4. Once problems are assigned, CMT draws arrows on the Stream Diagnostic Chart showing the interconnections among problems.
5. CMT analyzes resulting sets of problems, separates symptoms from core problems, and identifies problem stories and themes.
6. CMT creates an action plan specifically focusing on the core problems and themes and lays this action plan out on a Stream Planning Chart.
7. CMT implements the action plan.
8. As intervention process proceeds, CMT tracks change activity by posting it on a Stream Tracking Chart.

3

A Stream Organization Model

Changing an organization, normally a complex and challenging process, becomes more difficult when those instituting change operate without the guidance of a clear concept of the organization. People trying to change an organization need to know what its component parts are, how they are put together, and the effects that changing any one part may have on other parts as well as on the outputs of the system. Most experienced managers and consultants have distinct views of the critical factors to target for change. However, few use a comprehensive and integrated framework to guide their efforts, one that would provide a coherent perspective for smoothly executing complex change.

The purpose of this chapter is to present a broad diagnostic model of organizations, one that I have found useful in guiding my work with Stream Analysis. I call it the Stream Organization Model because it is rooted in the idea that organizations consist of a complex mixture of components, and that each of these components is a source of information influencing on-the-job behavior. This information continually flows through the system washing over each individual and leading to behavior that determines both organizational performance and personal development.

Readers very familiar with the literature on OD theory might want to skim this chapter. The material presented later can be understood without a thorough knowledge of the ideas discussed here. Although many of the concepts presented may not be new, there are some unique twists to old concepts and some ideas that have not been emphasized in previous writings on OD. For these reasons, I would urge the reader to at least review this material before proceeding to the following chapters.

Open Systems Theory

Organizations, as human systems, are open systems. They function by taking inputs such as people, raw materials, information, and technical knowledge, and transforming them into an output, product, or service that is distributed into the system's environment. System outputs generate resources from the environment, typically in the form of money, which are fed back and become part of the system's inputs. The environment acts on the organizational system in a variety of ways above and beyond the money it provides to pay for goods and services produced. This is one characteristic that makes the organization "open." It has permeable boundaries that allow things from the environment to pass through.

Aside from the exchange of resources, permeable organizational boundaries allow a second type of interaction with the environment to occur. Here, the organization is actively striving to connect with its environment and allow it to affect more closely the internal workings of the system. For example, many organizations are trying to find ways of getting closer to their customers; of developing favorable long-term relationships with suppliers or investors; of proactively recruiting the highest calibre people; of entering into joint ventures with other organizations; and so on. In all of these cases, the organization consciously makes its boundaries more permeable so as to create more effective transactions with the environment in which it exists.

One open systems view of organizations is shown in Fig. 3–1. In this representation, the organization is depicted in the broader environment with which it interacts. In addition to ex-

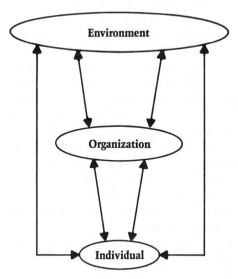

Figure 3-1
A Systems View of Organizations

isting in an external environment, the organization itself constitutes an environment for the people who work in it. Each individual, while in the organization, can be thought of as a unique system, existing in an environment (the work setting). The factors that collectively constitute the work environment for the individual employee are the basic components of the organization.

The broader environment also directly interacts with the individual organizational member. However, this typically occurs at the level of the individual, not at the level of the person as a member of the organizational setting. Nevertheless, the external environment still does affect the person on the job because people cannot turn off all that has happened to them outside when they walk through the doors of the organization.

The target organization shown in Fig. 3–1 could be a complete independent organization, or it could be a subpart of a larger one. As a subpart, it could range in size from a major division or department to a work group or section. Whatever one defines as the target organizational system, it interacts and exchanges resources with its environment. If the environment changes and makes new demands on the organization, then the organization must change and adapt if it is to remain viable over a long period of time. If the organization begins to behave differently in its environment (markets new products, begins buying other companies, hires lobbyists), then the environment is affected and also changes in response. The same type of argument can be made about the relationship between the individual and the organization or the individual and the external organizational environment. This is why Fig. 3–1 shows the arrows in all three of these cases going in both directions.[1]

Embedded in the organization is the system of individuals who make up the overall organization. It is important to isolate it because, as noted above, organizational change has truly occurred only when the people in the organization have changed the way they function in the work setting. Since this is a basic view on how change occurs in human systems, the next section elaborates this perspective.

Centrality of the Individual

All successful planned organizational change efforts ultimately lead to an organization's members changing the way they behave on the job, the decisions they make, the tasks they carry out, the information they share, the care with which they do their

---

[1]A key characteristic of open systems theory, that all effects typically go in both directions, is also a weakness in the practical use of the perspective. With everything influencing everything else, systems representations of organizations can become so complex that they are almost impossible to deal with. So, although the arrows are drawn in both directions for completeness, in all subsequent discussion I will assume that the main direction of influence is from the environment to the organization and from the organization to the individual.

work, the creativity they bring to their activities, the initiatives they take, and so on. Changes in such things as organization charts, cost control systems, budgetary systems, machinery, techniques for doing the job, policies and procedures, or job designs and responsibilities, will not have much impact on the outputs generated by the organization unless people behave differently as a result of these prescribed alterations. If the organization changes aspects of itself and its members do not change their basic work-related behaviors, then, in fact, there will be no positive long-term organizational change.

Now, this may seem like an obvious or naive statement, but I have found that unless the importance of people behaving differently is kept perfectly clear, change processes tend to lose focus and often become ineffective as a result. The purpose of planned change activity is to alter the behavior of organizational members so that they will more effectively perform needed tasks. As we will see later, this more effective performance of tasks leads to two important outcomes, one related to the organization and a second related to the individual organizational member.

Questions that immediately surface from this perspective are: "Just what behaviors are we talking about here? Which of them are most important? How do we define the most appropriate set?" Obviously, the number of critical behaviors can be quite large and can vary dramatically across organizational settings. Behaviors that might be important for one organization could well be less important in another.

Susan Hoffer and I explored this question in a study focused on finding out if there was a core set of effective behaviors that might be relatively constant across all organizational settings and, in addition, that might be associated with positive organizational outcomes.[2] In our research, we surveyed forty-two leading organization development scholars and practitioners in the United States, asking them to specify the behaviors they would see changed as a consequence of a successful planned change effort. Thirty-eight of the respondents agreed that there

---

[2]J. I. Porras and S. Hoffer, Common behavioral changes in successful organization development. *Journal of Applied Behavioral Science*, 1986, 22(4).

were behavior changes common to successful change efforts and were able to specify the ones they saw as most important.

The behaviors most frequently identified were organized into two sets. The first consisted of nine behaviors appropriate to all organizational members. The second focused specifically on managers, and included an additional five behaviors. Now, clearly, other behaviors besides the ones identified would be altered in any specific organizational change effort. However, those additional behaviors would be unique to the system, its needs, and the focus of its particular change activity. The behaviors described in the study represent a core set, ones hypothesized to change across all successful OD interventions in all types of change settings.

The key finding for our purposes here was that those individuals most knowledgeable in the field of organizational change believe that certain behavior and changes in them are commonly associated with system improvement. We can infer from this that activities which would lead to changes in on-the-job behaviors would also lead to improved organizational functioning with its consequent improvement in organizational outputs.

Let's explore this latter point more fully by discussing the relationship between changes in the behaviors of organizational members and changes in the outputs of the organizational system. Many in the planned change field have proposed that an organization generates outputs in two broad areas, one relating to the performance of the system and the second describing the personal development of each organizational member.[3] Each of these two organizational outputs will be discussed in relation to the behavioral change of individual organizational members.

Individual Behavior Change and Organizational Performance

Many factors contribute to the performance of an organization, but perhaps the most important and most difficult to influence is the behavior of each individual organizational member.

---

[3]A variety of authors have, in one way or another, specified these two as objectives of organization development efforts. Two examples are F. Friedlander and L. E. Brown, Organization development. *Annual Review of Psychology,* vol. 25 (1974):313–341, and E. F. Huse and T. G. Cummings, *Organization Development and Change,* 3rd ed. (St. Paul, Minn.: West, 1985).

Anyone who has worked in an organization knows that if people behave in ways such as working hard, taking responsibility and initiative, learning their jobs well, being creative, cooperating with one another, communicating what is important, listening to each other, facing conflict head on, committing themselves to their jobs, then the likelihood that the organization will perform well is enhanced. The organization may not turn out to be an economically successful system because of factors such as uncontrollable events in the environment or poor strategic choices made by its managers. But, given the context of its situation, if individual behaviors improve, the system will also tend to improve its performance.

A recent study by Hoffer investigated the relationship between the set of behaviors described in the previous section and the performance of a large real estate company.[4] Her study used a broad variety of measures to assess the performance of thirty-four relatively autonomous and geographically dispersed sales offices. Factors such as profits per salesperson, market share, and costs, were used to measure performance. The results showed a substantial and statistically significant relationship between each of the performance measures and a composite index reflecting a behavior profile for each office. The behavior profile was generated from a questionnaire, completed by each organizational member, asking them to assess the Porras and Hoffer study behaviors they saw occurring in their offices.

Based on these recent findings, it appears that a set of key behaviors does exist which are common to successful change efforts. Furthermore, it appears that these behaviors can be associated with high levels of organizational performance and that they, along with other, system-specific behaviors, are likely targets of any change effort.

Individual Behavior Change and Personal Development

Organizations generate a second set of outcomes, ones related to the personal well-being of their members. People are in-

---

[4]S. J. Hoffer, "Behavior and Organizational Performance: An Empirical Study." Unpublished doctoral dissertation, Graduate School of Business, Stanford University, 1986.

tellectually and psychologically affected by their involvement with the organization. In it, they gain new knowledge and skills and develop capabilities to deal with diverse tasks.

If the capabilities of individual organizational members are kept at a low level because, for example, their jobs are designed to be relatively simple, and their managers treat them in very authoritarian ways, offering few opportunities for training or promotion, then one would expect to see fairly simple on-the-job behavior. The workers would do what they were told (maybe), work minimum hours, contribute only what they were asked for (maybe), take little initiative, and so on. As a consequence, one would not expect to see much personal development. Instead, we could predict that the organizational members, as a group, would be relatively underdeveloped both intellectually and psychologically. They would not be growing in their ability to use whatever talents they possessed. Their confidence in themselves would not be growing and they would, more than likely, be making limited contributions to the success of the organization. They would not be learning how to improve their capabilities, both behavioral and technical. They would not be doing the many things that would lead to an actualization of their abilities and talents.

Unfortunately, at present I know of no research that links either behavior of people on the job with level of personal development, or changes in on-the-job behavior with personal growth. So, the view presented here is an assertion rather than one supported by empirical evidence. However, my experience working with many organizations has shown me that those individuals who are most actualized tend to exhibit many of the behaviors identified by the Porras and Hoffer study. This is another arena worthy of future investigation.

Figure 3–2 shows the relationships I have been describing. Up to now, I have proposed that the connections between behavior on the job and both organizational performance and personal development are unidirectional. In other words, behavior influences performance and development, but influence does not go in the opposite direction. Obviously, this is not the case, for often both the performance of the organization and the level of personal development affect behavior on the job. However, from the point of view of planned change I am developing here, the outcomes of

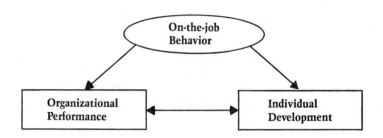

Figure 3–2
Individual Behavior and Organizational Outcomes

the organization cannot be changed directly. Rather, they are altered mainly as a result of the behavior changes that occur, which themselves are a consequence of the change efforts going on in the system. Since this is somewhat a chicken-or-egg problem, it is more consistent with our discussion to consider the forces acting in the direction shown in Fig. 3–2, all the time recognizing that they also go in the other direction.

There is a second relationship in Fig. 3–2 that should be amplified, the arrow showing a mutual effect between organizational performance and individual development. The assumption here is that these two outcomes affect each other; that over the long run one cannot improve without the other; and that, if an organization has placed great emphasis on one and virtually ignored the other, neither will occur.[5]

One final point should be made about the relationship between individual behavior change and changes in organizational performance and personal development. Up to now, I have not

---

[5]This is another area that, to my knowledge, has not been empirically investigated in long-term planned change projects. However, in numerous discussions I have had with managers from all levels of organizations involved in OD activities, the relationship proposed here is consistent with their experience.

distinguished among individuals at different hierarchical levels in the organization. Behavioral change in the chief executive officer would normally have a more substantial impact on overall organizational performance than changes in the behavior of one first level assembly-line worker. Yet, we should note that, for the greatest long-term systemwide change to occur, new CEO behaviors must eventually lead to new, more effective first line worker behaviors. Only when the entire system is behaving differently will overall performance change in the way I have been describing it.

Summary

In summary, then, people and their behaviors are key elements in understanding organizations and how to change them. Individual behavior is an important determinant in generating the organization's two chief outcomes — organizational performance and individual development. If one desires to improve the organization's outcomes, then the *behavior* of individual organizational members must be changed in desired directions.[6] We turn now to a view of how people learn new behaviors and change the way they act on the job.

How People Change

Since individual behavior change is the place we begin thinking about organizational outcome change, the first question one might ask is, "What does it take to get people in the organization to change their behaviors on the job?"[7] The answers are

---

[6]Regardless of the behavior of individual members, organizational outcomes constantly change merely because the environment has changed and responds differently to any given organizational output. The environment may have rewarded a particular organizational output at one point. At a later point, that same output may not receive the same positive response, thus changing the outcome for the organization. From our perspective here, we will omit these types of changes from our discussion and, instead, restrict ourselves to changes that result from deliberate attempts to improve organization functioning.

[7]Throughout the book, when I refer to individual on-the-job behavior I mean to include not only solitary behaviors, but also behaviors of individuals in interdependent situations — that is, behaviors in interpersonal situations, in group settings, and in intergroup settings.

numerous and diverse, as evidenced by the fact that the field of psychology has developed a vast array of theories and views of individual behavior change. As a result, agreement is not widespread about the best ways of getting people to change their behaviors in the work situation. However, during the last decade, a new theoretical perspective has been developed that has proven quite powerful in guiding behavior change with people experiencing various phobias. This approach, called *social cognitive theory*, emphasizes the thinking side of people and proposes a model describing the key factors driving people to make conscious choices about the behaviors they engage in.[8] Since much of effective behavior in organizations is rooted in people making choices about what they do, this particular approach provides a useful way of viewing change on the job.

For our purposes here, the most important assumptions of the social cognitive theory are 1) that people make conscious choices about their behaviors; 2) that the information people use to make their choices comes from their environment; and 3) that their choices are based on a) the things that are important to them, b) the views they have about their own abilities to behave in certain ways, and c) the consequences they think will accrue to whatever behavior they decide to engage in.[9] Before discussing each of these three criteria in more detail and emphasizing how they occur in an organizational setting, it would first be useful to say a few things about where people get the information they need to make choices.

The individual's environment is the most powerful source of information about behaviors and their consequences. As children, we all learned how to walk, talk, make facial expressions, use certain mannerisms, avoid certain things, and so on, by observing the world around us. We observed our parents, brothers,

---

[8] A. Bandura, *Social Learning Theory* (Englewood Cliffs, N.J.: Prentice-Hall, 1977), and A. Bandura, *Social Foundations of Thought and Action: A Social Cognitive Theory* (Englewood Cliffs, N.J.: Prentice-Hall, 1986).

[9] Social cognitive theory possesses many concepts similar to expectancy theory as proposed by such organizational scholars as Victor Vroom, Lyman Porter, and Ed Lawler. One of its most distinct differences, however, is its conceptualization of item 3b in the list of factors upon which people base their choice of behavior. This factor describes feelings of efficacy people have about themselves. Expectancy theory does not identify this phenomenon as a key factor and, in my opinion, suffers for it.

sisters, friends, relatives, anyone with whom we came in contact. We watched them, saw what they did, and what happened to them when they did it. It was through observations of others that we began to formulate a series of ideas about what behavior was acceptable and desirable and what was to be avoided. As adults, we become part of work organizations and continue to use these same processes for learning what is best to do. We observe what others are doing on the job and the consequences of the actions they take. We also are given many facts about how things are done or should be done in the work situation. All this information we use to decide how to behave on the job. The way that the information we receive affects our behavior is the process social cognitive theory seeks to model.

Let us focus on the third factor listed above as one of the key bases for choice about behaviors, people's beliefs about the consequences of any behavior in which they might engage. We all walk around with an incredibly complex set of views about the linkages between particular behaviors and the outcomes that result whenever those behaviors are used by someone. In terms of social cognitive theory these "views" are broadly labeled *outcome expectations.* We expect that certain things will happen as a consequence of specific actions. In terms of behavior change on the job, *the tighter the linkage between a particular behavior and a desired outcome, the more likely it is that we will engage in that behavior.*

I've used the term "desired outcome" in the statement above to imply that we attach a *value* to any outcome we see occurring in response to a particular behavior. Clearly, we do not desire everything equally. Some outcomes are extremely important to us and we will do anything within our power to achieve them. *The more desirable the outcome, the more likely we will engage in behavior we think will lead to it.*

The value of an outcome intertwines with our prediction of the likelihood that it will occur if we engage in certain behaviors. The two factors taken together help us decide whether or not to do something. They help us decide, but they are not the total picture. There is a third factor that social cognitive theory describes as a critical part of the process one goes through in deciding whether or not to engage in a particular behavior. That factor relates to another set of expectations we have. These focus on the predictions we make about whether or not we can actually perform the behavior in question and are called *efficacy expectations*, that is, expectations about the efficacy, or power, we feel about the behavior. In the organizational setting, we may feel more or less confident about our abilities to perform specific behaviors. *The more confident we are that we can actually assume a new behavior, the more likely we are to try it.*

Putting together the three key social cognitive theory factors—efficacy expectations, outcome expectations, and valences—we can see how in combination they determine whether or not people choose to engage in particular behaviors and whether or not they continue to behave in those ways over extended periods. No one of the three factors, by itself, can precipitate new behaviors from people. All three work in concert. However, the one factor that, if extremely high, can override lower levels in the other two, is *valence*. If people value some outcome very highly they may try to behave in ways to achieve it even though their relevant expectations may not be very high. On the other hand, high efficacy expectations or high outcome expectations cannot, by themselves, result in someone doing something. Individuals may have all the confidence in the world that they can perform some action, but if they don't believe that the action will lead to any worthwhile outcome, then they won't perform it. Likewise, if a person is convinced that a particular behavior will lead to a specific outcome, but doesn't value the outcome, then he or she won't engage in the behavior either.

In the real world, things are not so simple. First and foremost, outcomes are often quite ambiguous. People might not have a clear idea of what they want, or they may know what they want but may not see specific behaviors or a concrete outcome relating to their desires. To complicate things even further, particular behaviors can lead to more than one outcome; any one outcome can be achieved by more than one behavior; or both sets of relationships can be at work. No one can analyze a real life situation completely, so I'm not proposing that any person involved with individual behavior change in organizations try. The thing that is important about all of this is to realize that these factors are operating in individuals and that they are influenced by what they perceive is going on in their work environment. In order to change people's behavior on the job, therefore, it is necessary to change the environment in which they work.

Figure 3–3 contains these new concepts added on to the model we have been developing. The organizational work setting sends messages to the individual that affect his or her efficacy

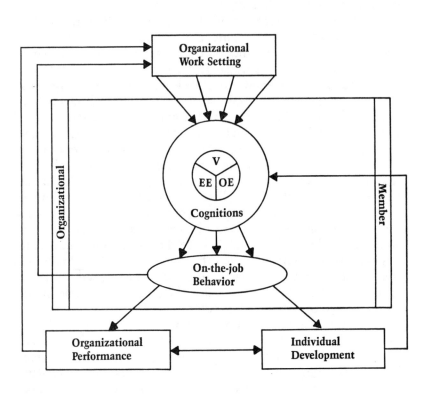

Key

V = **Valence**
EE = **Efficacy Expectation**
OE = **Outcome Expectation**

Figure 3–3
Relationships among Work Setting, the Individual, and Outcomes

expectations, outcome expectations, and valences. Based on their impact, the person chooses to engage in a variety of behaviors on the job which then contribute to the level of performance of the organization and the level of each individual organizational member's personal development. Several feedback loops exist in which both on-the-job behavior and organization performance affect the work setting and in which individual development can alter the organizational member's cognition. Reverse effects between behavior, cognition, and work setting exist, but for clarity are not shown.

Based on this perspective are several key questions for those wishing to change organizations by changing the behavior of people in them: What are the factors in the internal organizational environment that influence people's efficacy expectations, outcome expectations, or valences? How do these factors contribute to dysfunctional behavior on the job? Can we organize these factors in such a way that we can meaningfully influence them? In essence, what the questions are asking for is a model of organizations that can be used both to diagnose problems and to guide corrective action. We will turn to just such a model, one I have used in the Stream Analysis approach.

Components of the Model

The Stream Organization Model has been developed specifically for those who wish to change organizations and who need some theoretical perspective to guide them. Drawn from the existing organizational change literature, a decade and a half of research on the effects of planned organizational change efforts, and intervention experiences in various change settings, this framework attempts to balance the complexity of organizational life with the simplicity needed to make it readily usable with the stream charting technique.

Dimensions of the Work Setting

The previous discussion broadly described an organization using systems terms and presented a social cognitive theory analysis of how people change their behaviors. Both systems theory and social cognitive theory emphasize the concept of environment. This concept will be used as a place to begin building the Stream Organizational Model, which will focus not on the external environment of the organization, but rather on the internal environment that the organization creates for the people who work in it. As noted earlier, the work setting[10] is critical in the behavior change process because it sends organizational members the signals that affect their expectations (both efficacy and outcome) and the valences they attach to various personal outcomes.

What, then, is an organization's work environment like when its members walk into it every day? What are they bombarded with? What are the messages they get about what they should be doing? What are they required to do by their formal job description? What are they told to do by their supervisors? What are they rewarded for doing? What are they punished for doing? What behaviors are ignored? What limitations exist as a consequence of the physical space they work in? What behavior does the machinery and equipment they work with demand of them?

These are but a few of the numerous questions one could ask about the setting in which people work. The answers to questions such as these identify key factors in the internal organizational environment that shape and guide behavior of people on the job. The same factors would be pointed to by social cognitive theory as needing to be altered because they provide the signals that influence the expectations and values of people in the system. Let us specify exactly what these factors might be.[11]

---

[10]Throughout this discussion, I will use the terms *internal organizational environment, work environment, organizational setting,* and *work setting* interchangeably.

[11]In the development of these ideas we have been influenced by a wide variety of organizational diagnostic models. Most notable are the following works. P. F. Drucker, *Management: Tasks — Responsibilities — Practice.* (New York: Harper & Row, 1974). F. E. Emery and E. L. Trist, Analytical model for sociotechnical systems. In W. A. Pasmore and J. J. Sherwood, eds., *Sociotechnical Systems: A Sourcebook* (San Diego: University Associates, 1978):120–131. W. L. French and C. H. Bell, *Organization Development: Behavioral Science Interventions for Organization Improvement,* 3rd ed. (Englewood Cliffs, N.J.: Prentice-Hall, 1984). P. R. Lawrence and J. W. Lorsch, *Developing Organizations: Diagnosis and Action* (Reading, Mass.: Addison-Wesley, 1969). D. A. Nadler and M. L. Tushman, A diagnostic model for organizational behavior. In J. R. Hackman, E. E. Lawler, and L. W. Porter, eds., *Perspectives on Behavior in Organizations* (New York: McGraw-Hill, 1977). F. Steele, *Physical Settings and Organization Development* (Reading, Mass.: Addison-Wesley, 1973). M. R. Weisbord, *Organizational Diagnosis: A Workbook of Theory and Practice* (Reading, Mass.: Addison-Wesley, 1978).

An organization can be thought of as being built on a foundation of four basic dimensions. Taken together, they constitute the specific factors in the work setting. Since the work setting is the environment in which people work, and since the environment plays a key role in determining the behavior of people, these four dimensions define for us the things that, if changed, will wind up changing the expectations and valences of people and, as a consequence, their on-the-job behaviors. The four foundational areas, or streams, of the organization are the 1) Organizing Arrangements, 2) Social Factors, 3) Technology, and 4) Physical Setting. These are dimensions of the broad process through which system inputs are transformed into system outputs. Table 3–1 lists the four organizational streams and their elements.[12] Each will be briefly described in the following sections.

Organizing Arrangements

The Organizing Arrangements (OA) stream contains all the parts of the organization that are set up to coordinate formally both the behavior of people and the functioning of various parts of the organization. It is the formal side of the organization, the side usually existing in some sort of written form. It represents a description of the way the organization is supposed to work, not necessarily the way it actually does. The Organizing Arrangements stream consists of the following components:

Goals. The guiding forces for all OA of a system are the goals of the organization, what it is trying to achieve. Formal goals are usually spelled out and reviewed at least once per year. Goals exist at all organizational levels, from top to bottom. They are more likely to be written at higher levels, yet they can and often do exist in a written form at the lower levels. Goals guide behavior

---

[12]The factors I describe here are not new and, in fact, are well known to all who have worked in or studied organizations. Furthermore, the dimensions into which we group the factors have also been previously identified, but they have been operationally defined in a somewhat different manner than the way I have done it here. What is new is the particular combination of factors clustered into each dimension, the role ascribed to these factors in influencing the behavior of individuals on the job, and the relationships I propose exist across the various parts of the model.

Table 3-1
Description of Organizational Components in the Stream Organization Model

1. Organizing Arrangements

A. Goals
B. Strategies
C. Formal Structure
D. Administrative Policies and Procedures
E. Administrative Systems
F. Formal Reward Systems
   1. Evaluation System
   2. Pay Systems
   3. Benefits Packages

2. Social Factors

A. Culture
   1. Basic Assumptions
   2. Values
   3. Norms
   4. Language and Jargon
   5. Rituals
   6. History
   7. Stories
   8. Myths
   9. Symbols
B. Interaction Processes
   1. Interpersonal
   2. Group
   3. Intergroup
C. Social Patterns and Networks
   1. Communication
   2. Problem Solving/Decision Making
   3. Influence
   4. Status
D. Individual Attributes
   1. Attitudes and Beliefs
   2. Behavioral Skills
   3. Feelings

3. Technology

A. Tools, Equipment, and Machinery
B. Technical Expertise
C. Job Design
D. Work Flow Design
E. Technical Policies and Procedures
F. Technical Systems

4. Physical Settings

A. Space Configuration
   1. Size
   2. Shape
   3. Relative Locations
B. Physical Ambiance
   1. Light
   2. Heat
   3. Noise
   4. Air Quality
   5. Cleanliness
C. Interior Design
   1. Decorations
   2. Furniture
   3. Window Coverings
   4. Floor Coverings
   5. Colors
      a. Floors
      b. Walls
      c. Ceilings
D. Architectural Design

Source: G. E. Germane, *The Executive Course,* © 1986, Addison-Wesley Publishing Company, Inc., Reading, Massachusetts, Page 266, Table 8.1.

if they force individual decision makers to assess their decisions in light of their contribution to the formally espoused goals of the organization.

Strategies. Closely linked with goals are strategies. Organizational strategies lay out the ways of achieving system goals. Their importance cannot be overemphasized. Choice of strategy plays a critical role in the success of any system but is especially important for those organizations existing in rapidly changing environments. In the latter case, a well thought out strategy can keep the organization from being unnecessarily confused about what it wants to do as well as help keep it poised to take maximum advantage of any opportunity that might arise as a consequence of environmental shifts.

There are many different types of strategies. Some are externally oriented and have to do with such things as choice of markets, products to develop, advertising approaches to use, and so forth. Others, more internally oriented, might focus on types of people to hire, career development approaches, management development approaches, and reward systems. As with goals, strategies can exist at all levels of the organization. Those at the top, dealing with the system as a whole, tend to be more formal and may take a written form. Those at the bottom often exist as an intuitive ideology.

Formal Structure. Probably the most common part of the OA area is the organization chart, or the formal structure of the organization. It defines the authority relationships — who reports to whom, who is at the top of the organization and has the most authority, who is at the bottom and has the least. It also defines the broad roles of each part of the organization and specifies the formal flows of communication. Historically, the organization chart has been the major target for those trying to change organizations.

Administrative Policies and Procedures. Policies and procedures are a fourth component of the OA stream. They consist of the formal rules that define "ways of doing things" in the organization. They are set up to guide people's behavior so that everything is coordinated and nothing falls through the cracks. Some organizations attempt to cover most aspects of life in the system with a policy or procedure. Others formally define very few of the rules for operating in the organization and getting things done.

Administrative Systems. The administrative systems are all the formally designed and established systems focused on facilitating the coordination of the organization. These include such systems as financial accounting and control systems, information systems, personnel management systems. This area of organizations is also a quite common target of change efforts.

Reward Systems. The formal reward system, technically an administrative system, is described separately because of its unique importance and the more direct impact it has on the behavior of individuals in the organization. The reward system includes the performance evaluation system, the pay system, and the benefits system.

Summary. The main Organizing Arrangements are the most typical targets of planned change efforts. As formal aspects of the system, they send signals about what people in the system are supposed to be doing. Goals tell them what the organization is trying to achieve and define what each individual should be shooting for. Strategies prescribe the way the organization is to go about achieving its goals and broadly circumscribe the behaviors most desired by the organization. Structure tells people the role of their unit and the authority relationships. Policies and procedures tell individuals that they can or cannot do certain things in the work setting. Administrative systems provide information, coordinate data, and develop the resources needed to implement strategy. And finally, the reward system assesses and rewards people for their contributions to the success of the system in achieving its goals.

What I have described up to now is the way the system is *supposed* to work, the formal side of the organization. It is the side that assumes rationality and individual behavior consistent with rational choices. It sends messages to people telling them how they are supposed to behave. If all its components were aligned and consistent with one another, then the messages sent out by them would all reinforce the same behaviors and exert a rather powerful force.

Although we all recognize that people do not always respond consistently with what the OA stream of variables tells them to do, aspects of the organization such as the reward system and the formal structure do have a substantial impact on the behavior of people. Yet organizational members respond in many different ways, some of them quite unpredictable, and they do so for a variety of reasons. Some of these reasons are rooted in the fact that there are other key areas of the organization which also have powerful effects on people and their behavior. We turn now to one of those areas, the Social Factors of the organization.

Social Factors

Social Factors (SF) encompass all things directly related to people in the organization: their characteristics (individually and in small groups), their patterns and processes of interaction, and their features as larger social groups. This stream has traditionally been called the informal organization in contrast to the Organizing Arrangements, which have been considered the formal side. It has several components.

Culture. The culture of organizations has been a popular topic in management literature over the past few years. Many scholars and practitioners are focusing on culture as the key area for change activity[13] and are finding it a difficult and complex phenomenon to understand, much less change.

To give the reader a flavor for the number of different ways the concept has been approached, culture has been described in terms of artifacts, basic assumptions, beliefs, collective will, core

---

[13]Some of the more recent and useful books on culture are the following: S. M. Davis, *Managing Corporate Culture* (Cambridge, Mass.: Ballinger, 1984). T. E. Deal and A. A. Kennedy, *Corporate Cultures* (Reading, Mass.: Addison-Wesley, 1982). R. H. Kilmann, M. J. Saxton, and R. Serpa, eds., *Managing Corporate Cultures* (San Francisco: Jossey-Bass, 1985). V. Sathe, *Managerial Action and Corporate Culture* (Homewood, Ill.: Irwin, 1985). E. H. Schein, *Organizational Culture and Leadership* (San Francisco: Jossey-Bass, 1985).

values, ideologies, important understandings, norms, observed behavioral regularities, philosophies, practices, and themes of content. More recent views of organizational culture have both deepened and broadened the concept. The concept is deepened by considering culture as rooted in the deep and largely unconscious implicit assumptions that organizational members hold, and it is broadened in the sense that almost all aspects of organizational life are seen to be largely driven by culture.[14]

Edgar Schein defines culture as

> a pattern of basic assumptions — invented, discovered, or developed by a given group as it learns to cope with its problems of external adaptation and internal integration — that has worked well enough to be considered valid and, therefore, to be taught to new members as the correct way to perceive, think, and feel in relation to those problems.[15]

Culture then begins with basic assumptions about the world. These assumptions evolve into central values which then dictate the development of artifacts or the constructed social environment.[16] Below, we will briefly describe the two main components of culture which derive from the basic assumptions held by organizational members.

Central values provide the operating principles that members of the organization use to guide their behavior. Webster defines values as the social principles, goals, or standards held or

---

[14]See Schein, *Organizational Culture and Leadership*, and J. Martin and D. Meyerson, Organizational cultures and the denial, channeling, and acceptance of ambiguity, Research Report No. 807R, Research Paper Series, Graduate School of Business, Stanford University, July 1986, for detailed arguments for this point of view.

[15]Schein, *Organizational Culture and Leadership*, p. 9.

[16]This broad paradigm is drawn from Schein, ibid., with some key modifications. Schein describes artifacts as consisting of the constructed social and physical environment. In my view, both the social and physical environments must be considered in a somewhat more limited sense than prescribed by Schein. Social environment factors such as interaction processes, social patterns and networks, and task-oriented social processes are treated as separate parts of the Social Factors stream. On the physical environment side, I see these artifacts limited to their more symbolic meaning and not considered in their broader context. The broader aspects of the physical side of the organization are included in the Physical Setting stream described later.

accepted by an individual, class, society, etc. Every organization has a set of values that influences the behaviors of people on the job. Clearly, organizations do not hold a single value, nor even a small number. Usually organizations espouse a series of values, some of which may, at times, contradict others. In cases such as these, trade-offs must be made in an attempt to maximize as many of the values as possible while at the same time making certain that the most important values are not compromised. This ideal cannot always be achieved. Nonetheless, much of what top managers do is to make decisions that help the organization to behave as consistently with as many of its values as possible.

I should be careful to point out that what organizations say their values are is not necessarily reflected in their behavior. Values that are espoused are often ideals. It is the behavior of the organization that must be observed and the true values guiding it inferred from the observed acts of organizational members, especially managers.

Values are translated into reality through the development of *artifacts* — the social and physical environment constructed by organizational members to guide their behavior. The components of social environment take many forms. *Norms*, perhaps the most powerful factor in the social environment, grow directly out of values. They are "the rules of the game," informal guidelines on how to behave. Norms tell people what they are supposed to be doing, wearing, saying, believing, what is "O.K." and what is taboo, what to look out for and what to ignore, how to see things and how to interpret what you see. Norms are not written, for if they were, they would be formal policies or procedures.

Norms are passed on to new employees by word of mouth or behaviors and are enforced by the way people in the organization respond when a norm is broken or violated. This is one very powerful way that human beings have of influencing one another. We control others by the way we react to them. Some people respond very readily to this type of control, some do not, but in any case, it is going on in all social situations and it is a mechanism through which social systems can keep themselves functioning. Norms provide the basis out of which social control is exercised.

Values are also transmitted to an organization through several other social constructions such as language or jargon, rituals, history, stories, and myths. Organizational *jargon* is the shorthand language developed by organizational members to communicate rich meaning in simple or coded terms. *Rituals* are ceremonial acts that convey organizational values as well as information about the functioning of the system. They can vary in nature from very solemn to quite irreverent. Yet each ritual serves a particular function and collectively they serve to strengthen the culture of the organization. The *history* of the organization is the broad collection of facts about what the organization has accomplished. It tends to be factual in nature and wide in scope. It conveys where the organization has been and, as such, describes the values and norms in a more general way.

Stories are a part of history, but they tend to be more focused, contain more emotional undertones, and have a closer link to the value or values they are intended to convey. Stories serve a very powerful function; they tell the people in the system how we operate, who we are, what we do, what is important to do and what is important not to do. By being able to convey information like this, new people in the organization are made more comfortable and they begin to fit into the organization more rapidly. *Myths* are like stories, but they take bits and pieces of factual data and weave them together. They are fictitious but have a strong basis in the reality of the organization. They are usually quite powerful in zeroing in on the particular message to be conveyed. They often have a heroic flavor, focusing on the successes of key individuals and how the values of the organization contributed to their accomplishments and to the organization.

The second general class of cultural artifact, *physical constructs*, consists primarily of the symbols created by organizational members to convey the values of the system. They translate into some concrete physical reality, the things that are important. Fifty-year pins reflect the value of long-term loyalty to the organization; corner offices with windows convey high status; plaques show that something worthy of recognition was achieved by an individual or unit; and so on. Organizations can create numerous symbols to remind their members that certain things are important.

In summary, through norms, jargon, rituals, history, stories, myths, and symbols the organization's values are transmitted to its members. The more of these mechanisms that exist in the system, the more consistent the behavior of people in the organization. As the number of cultural messages about what one is supposed to do or not do increases (given that these messages are more or less consistent or complementary), then it becomes very clear in people's minds exactly what is acceptable and not acceptable, and they tend to behave accordingly. This is not to say that everyone will be behaving exactly the same. It does imply, however, that there will tend to be less variation in people's behavior in this situation than if the number of messages delivered by the culture were smaller.

One final aspect of culture cuts across many ideas — the notion of management or leadership style. The basic assumptions and values of managers have a key impact on the concrete decisions they make and, through many of those decisions, influence the culture of the overall organization. In addition, managers' assumptions and values strongly influence their own behavior when dealing with others. Through these two processes, the decisions they make and the behavior they exhibit, managers create a style for themselves that in turn affects the organization's culture. Organizational culture is much more than management style but perhaps there is nothing that helps more to broadly determine culture than management style.

A fundamental difference exists between the perspective on culture reflected here and other views of this factor currently popular in organization literature. Many theorists conceive of culture as being at the root of most, if not all, organizational variables. They believe that typical organizational variables such as strategy, goals, or administrative procedures are mainly manifestations, if not actual components, of the culture of the organization. My view is that variables such as these are highly interconnected with culture but are not the same as or a part of culture. They are variables at the same level of substance and importance as culture and are highly influenced by it, but they are clearly separate and unique from it. It is important to emphasize that high levels of *interdependence* (not just dependence) generally exist between an organization's culture and other organizational factors so that, just as culture can drive them, they also can partially determine what the culture looks like.

Interaction Processes. People work together to perform the tasks of the organization. In doing so, they interact in various social groupings: interpersonal, group, and intergroup. In each of these three levels of social groupings, human interactions take place. What kind of information do an organization's members share and how do they transmit and receive it? Are people arguing all the time? How do they resolve their differences? Does conflict occur? How is it resolved? In what ways are problems solved? How do decisions get made? Are major decisions made differently from minor ones? These interactions are characterizable in many ways, for example as communication processes, conflict resolution processes, problem-solving processes, and decision-making processes. These processes are but a few aspects of what goes on when people interact.

The culture of the organization affects interactions and vice versa. The organization's norms may guide how a management team might work on a problem. How management works on a problem can do a lot to establish the norms of the organization, especially if the management team consists of the CEO and direct subordinates. Nevertheless, these processes can be viewed as social factors in their own right, separate from the culture of the organization. They are more directly amenable to change than culture. People can be taught different, more effective ways to behave in interactive situations. They can be made aware of the dynamics that occur when people interact and can be taught to change them when they see them being ineffective.

Social Patterns and Networks. The organization chart specifies the formal patterns of communication, decision making, and authority. An informal set of patterns exists that modifies the way things are supposed to be done. Informal patterns and networks of communication, problem solving or decision making, influence, and status exist which, at times, are consistent with the formal structure of the organization and, at times, are at odds with it.

People in very separate parts of the organization may be in constant contact with one another. Decision making and problem solving may occur in ways not specified by the policies and procedures manual. Individuals with exceptional technical knowledge may be more influential than others higher up in the organizational hierarchy. Even though they are not supposed to, some people may have access to information of value to other organizational members and, by sharing it, may exercise substantial influence over what goes on.

Status patterns typically are direct offshoots of the patterns of communication, problem solving or decision making, and influence in an organization. Individuals with great expertise, people who are at the hub of communication flows, individuals or groups who, in reality, make key decisions are all afforded a level of status not necessarily reflected in the formal organizational structure.

These informal patterns and networks display themselves in the context of the formal structures, policies, and procedures. If Social Factors are highly consistent with and mutually reinforcing of the Organizing Arrangements, the organization will tend to run more smoothly and effectively. If the two are highly inconsistent or contradictory, then one could expect substantial inefficiency in the system. Much energy would be spent by some people trying to enforce the formal dimensions of the organization, while at the same time others would be investing at least an equal amount of energy developing ways to get their jobs done in spite of the formal part.

Individual Attributes. The final component of the Social Factors stream describes the attributes of the individual organizational member. People walk into the organization with certain attitudes and beliefs that they have developed in a variety of ways and over long periods of time. In addition they possess a repertoire of behaviors that have succeeded for them in the past. As they express their beliefs, attitudes, and feelings, either verbally or through their behavior, they affect the behavior of all those around them.

Each person's beliefs about the organization (for example, whether it is a fair place to work, whether it deals with its employees honestly, whether it can be trusted), and about how people should work together (being cooperative, taking responsibility, taking initiative, being willing to compromise) influence how others behave in response. Also influential are people's beliefs about their relationships with managers (Do what you are told, Do what you want when the boss is not around, Help the boss out as much as you can) and about any other factor related to life at work. Attitudes such as liking one's work, the organization, or co-workers ultimately have an effect on those around one. Together, these two sets of individual attributes influence, not only the way an individual performs in the organization, but also the way others around him or her behave.

The beliefs and attitudes of interest here are the ones held by each organizational member individually, and are separate from the broadly held ones that are part of the organization's culture. It is important to consider, also, how beliefs and attitudes of employees relate to the way jobs are designed and how people are expected to work together. These attributes of the individual must match the intended organizational design or inefficiencies are introduced into the system and ineffective operation typically results.

A third key individual attribute is the feelings held by people in the organization. Feelings influence the ways people see their organizational situation and the way they wind up responding to it. Until recently, feelings were not valued as important factors in organizational functioning. Efforts were made by almost all managers to "stick to business" and leave feelings out of any conversation having to do with getting the job done. Today, there is a much greater awareness of feelings and the impact they have on an organization's performance. Feelings are more commonly seen as additional data points, information that should be introduced into and considered in any important decision requiring the strong commitment of people in the effective implementation of that decision.

A fourth important attribute of individual organizational members is the behavioral skills they possess. By behavioral skills I mean the ability an individual has to interact effectively with others. Is the individual able to listen well, can he or she communicate effectively, show support for co-workers, be open to other's ideas, be flexible, deal with conflict, tolerate ambiguity in the work situation? The more behaviorally skillful the members of the organization, the greater the system's capacity to adapt and change in response to new environmental demands.

Summary. The four Social Factors — culture, interaction processes, informal patterns and networks, and individual attributes — describe the human and informal side of the organization. They are often the most intangible, the softest or "mushiest" parts of the organization and the most difficult to characterize or pin down. Yet, as I will discuss later, they heavily influence the three other dimensions of the organization. The degree to which a Social Factors component such as culture permeates and affects the design of components in other streams is currently a popular topic of both theory and research. The view I take here is that culture is heavily interconnected to other organizational factors but is conceptually separate from them and should be considered a unique organizational variable.

From the description of the Social Factors stream one might expect that these factors are the most difficult aspect of the organization to change, and they are. No easy, clear-cut formulas exist for convincingly altering these facets of the organization. Yet, the more aware one is of them and the more one can think systematically about them, the more likely it is that one can influence them, especially in concert with other changes being made in the organization.

Technology

The Technology stream of the organization encompasses all of the factors that directly enter into the transformation of organizational inputs into organizational outputs. The organizational dimension of Technology therefore describes a wide array of variables: 1) the tools, equipment, and machinery used in the transformation process, 2) designs of jobs required to perform that transformation, 3) work flow design, 4) technical procedures, 5) technical systems, and 6) technical expertise of organizational members.[17]

Tools, Equipment, and Machinery. The tools, equipment, and machinery required to produce the organization's products can vary greatly. This component of the Technology stream can range from something as large and complex as a mainframe computer, a metal parts stamping machine, a hot steel rolling machine, or a drill press, to a tool as simple as a pencil. Any physical object that can be used to perform a function on something else in the creation of a product or service is part of the Technology of the organization. The tools, equipment, and machinery used in the organization can prescribe, guide, facilitate, limit, or precipitate behaviors of individual employees.

Job Design. The designs of jobs are a second important component of the Technology stream. Jobs are designed by putting a series of tasks together into a package called a job. The number of tasks to be done as part of the job may be small or large, the complexity of each task to be performed may be low or high, there may be high or low variety in the task, the employee may be more or less autonomous in performing them, the speed in which the tasks must be performed may be low or high, and so on.

Some consequences of designing jobs that require a broad range of skills, knowledge, and creativity are that typically people doing those jobs tend to be more productive, more involved in their work, less likely to be absent or to leave the company, and more committed to contributing their best efforts to the organization.

Work Flow Design. Jobs are grouped together to create a flow of work. Products are created by grouping jobs in certain

---

[17]These dimensions were drawn from a wide variety of sources; however, of greatest influence were the following works. J. R. Hackman and G. R. Oldham, *Work Redesign* (Reading, Mass.: Addison-Wesley, 1980). C. L. Hulin and M. Roznowski, Organizational technologies: effects on organizations' characteristics and individuals' responses. In L. L. Cummings and B. Staw, *Research in Organizational Behavior*, vol. 7 (Greenwich, Conn.: JAI Press, 1985), pp. 39–85. E. Trist, The evolution of socio-technical systems: a conceptual framework and an action research program. *Issues in the Quality of Working Life*, A series of occasional papers, Ontario Quality of Working Life Centre, No. 2, June 1981.

ways and merging the outputs of those jobs in such a manner that an end product is produced. How jobs are grouped together can do much to determine the effectiveness of the overall production process.

Designs of work flow are based on the type of task interdependence that exists in getting work done. Three types exist.[18]

1. Sequential interdependence, in which task A provides the input for task B
2. Reciprocal interdependence, in which A provides the input for B and vice versa
3. Pooled interdependence, in which A and B both provide input for the whole and each is supported by the whole.

Knowledge of the types of interdependence that exist in producing a product guides design of the work flow.

Technical Expertise. Level of knowledge and the physical skills, which allow an employee to carry out the concrete tasks necessary to perform his or her assigned job, define the technical expertise aspect of the Technology stream. If organizational members do not possess the actual knowledge and skills necessary to perform their jobs, then it does not matter how interesting or well designed the jobs are, they will not be done at the levels desired by the organization.

Technical Procedures. In order to perform the tasks of transforming the system's inputs into its outputs, certain procedures must be followed in working with the tools, equipment, and machinery; in dealing with the raw materials (in a manufacturing operation); in dealing with customers or clients (in a service organization); and generally in doing whatever is necessary to accomplish the job assigned. These procedures are called technical procedures. To contrast them with the administrative procedures described as Organizing Arrangements, these are directly related to the transformation process and are not broadly organizational in nature. They usually derive from engineering design specifications and define how the job is supposed to be done.

---

[18]J. D. Thompson, *Organizations in Action* (New York: McGraw-Hill, 1967), p. 54.

Technical Systems. The systems that provide information about the state of the transformation process, or control aspects of it, are called technical systems. Scheduling systems, parts control systems, procurement systems, inventory control systems, maintenance systems, "just-in-time" systems, are all examples of technical systems. They provide the technical structure on which coordination and management of the transformation process can occur.

Summary. Technology has been the most dominant dimension of organizational design since the inception of the modern industrial organization. The factors that make up technology have quite direct effects on individual organizational member behavior. The design and content of one's job has perhaps a more powerful impact on people than any other aspect of the organization. The more dominant and well defined the Technology of a system, the more impact it has on individual behavior. Therefore, understanding the various components of the Technology stream and the ways in which they affect individuals is a prerequisite for successful organizational change.

Physical Setting

The final key organizational stream is the Physical Setting. Those familiar with the classic Hawthorne studies will recall that they were originally designed to study the effects of physical setting conditions, such as the lighting, on employees. However, for several decades there has been relatively little interest in understanding the effects of the physical environment on the people who work in them. This side of organizations has been receiving more attention recently as a result of renewed academic and practitioner interest.[19] Recent studies by Hatch,[20] Becker,[21] and Allen

---

[19]J. Pfeffer, The physical setting. Class presentation, Executive Program in Organizational Change, Graduate School of Business, Stanford University, July 1986. F. Steele, The ecology of executive teams: A new view of the top. *Organizational Dynamics*, vol. 11, no. 4 (1983):65–78.

[20]M. J. Hatch, The Organization as a Physical Environment of Work: Physical Structure Determinants of Task Attention and Interaction. Unpublished Doctoral Dissertation, Graduate School of Business, Stanford University, 1985.

[21]F. Becker, *Workspace: Creating Environments in Organizations* (New York: Praeger, 1981).

and Fusfeld[22] have highlighted the relationships between selected Physical Setting variables and other organizational variables such as productivity, task attention, satisfaction, communication, and interaction. In addition, the increased application of systems theory, as a comprehensive way of thinking about organizations, has led to the rekindling of interest in the physical setting and its effects on behaviors of organizational members.

The Physical Setting includes the concrete structures and objects of the nonsocial/nontechnical part of the environment in which people work. Based on the body of research and theory cited above, I have identified a series of factors as most important. Some of them have direct impact on specific behaviors in the organization, while others affect attitudes more directly, making their relation to behaviors less clear. Because of this, I will describe some factors in greater detail than others, choosing to emphasize mainly those which have the greatest direct impact on behavior. The four main components of the Physical Setting dimension are the 1) space configuration, 2) physical ambiance, 3) interior design, and 4) overall architectural design.

Space Configuration. The way an organization's work space is laid out affects the way people work in that space. The amount of space people have to work in influences what they do, both in the physical restrictions that limit or channel what a person can do, as well as in the psychological effects it can have. Debate often rages over the merits of open office designs. Aside from the economic benefits of open offices, advocates most often point to the increased communication that can occur in these space configurations. Detractors emphasize noisiness and lack of privacy as its main limitations. Open or closed offices have different effects on the ways people do their work. The key is to create a physical design that most appropriately matches the type of work to be done and the ways people must work to accomplish their tasks most effectively.

Shape of space relates not only to horizontal shape but also to vertical shape. Vertical shape refers to the height of walls and

---

[22]T. J. Allen and A. R. Fusfeld, Design for communication in the research and development lab. *Technology Review* (May 1976):65–71.

partitions. Of most importance here is whether or not walls or partitions exist that go all the way up to the ceiling and how high partitions might be. Walls provide privacy. That's the good news! The bad news is that they also create isolation. Both privacy and opportunity for interaction are necessary in any well-functioning organization. Creating space that will provide both in the right amounts to the right people is a critical task for any space designer.

Relative location of offices or work areas is perhaps the most critical factor in space design. Where people are located does much to determine to whom they talk, with whom they build relationships, to whom they might go for help or advice, with whom they share information about their jobs, whom they trust, with whom they are willing to cooperate, whom they might help, for whom they might go out of their way, and many other large and small factors that affect the way people get both their work and the organization's work done.

Communicating face-to-face may have an impact quite different from communicating over the telephone. Communication on the telephone, first of all, tends to occur less frequently than face-to-face communication, it tends to be less detailed, and it usually is less satisfying because the individual cannot read the signals that the other person is giving out in response to what is being said. So, proximity of offices has a strong effect on the quality of people's work together.

Physical Ambiance. A second aspect of the Physical Setting is concerned with the characteristics of the ambiance such as the quantity and types of lights, the level of heat or cold, the levels and types of noise, the quality of air people breathe, and the cleanliness of the area in which they work. All these are what Herzberg has called hygienic factors. By themselves they do not motivate people to work harder or better. Instead, they facilitate or make possible high levels of performance.

Interior Design. This third component of the Physical Setting describes the furniture, decorations, window and floor coverings, and colors of floors, walls, and ceilings. Most people use both social and physical cues from their surroundings to figure out what others think about them and then factor that information into what they think about themselves. Therefore, the quality, style, and design of settings in which people work can influence the way they see themselves and their roles.

When people are allowed to influence the design of their immediate surroundings, they typically feel more a part of the system and respond accordingly. A simple example occurs in situations in which people are allowed to decorate their work stations or offices with personal effects such as pictures, posters, and plants. This personalization of the work environment results in different attitudes toward the organization and their role in it.

Architectural Design. The architectural design describes the overall structural design of the buildings in which people work. Much the same comment can be made about the impact of the architectural design on individual behavior as was made about the interior design. An important additional effect is felt because of the more massive impact of the overall building design on a person's perceptions of the organization. Contrast the views one might have of a machine shop located in a forty-year-old building in the middle of a decaying inner city with an insurance company housed in a three-year-old building in the suburbs. Attitudes about being part of either of these two organizations would differ across many dimensions. This is not to imply that the way machine shop employees might feel about their organization would be better or worse than the way insurance company employees might feel about theirs. It does mean that their feelings would likely be different and would need to be understood when attempting to change the architectural design as a way of improving the system's functioning.

In summary, the Physical Setting within which people work can do much to block or facilitate effective organizational behavior. Generally, it does not appear to have a substantial motivational impact on people. That is, it does not make people want to do this or that, but rather, if an individual is inclined to behave in a certain way in the organization, the Physical Setting can make that behavior easier or harder to perform. In this way, workers' and managers' effectiveness may be enhanced or reduced. Space configuration is perhaps the most significant aspect of the

Physical Setting and, as such, must be designed with an eye toward using it to support the designs of the other three streams.

Summary

Overall, then, four organizational dimensions or streams (Organizing Arrangements, Social Factors, Technology, and Physical Setting) make up the internal processes of the organization. They must be designed so as to best deal with the environmental demands placed on the organization while, at the same time, create work setting conditions that will best support effective on-the-job behaviors of organizational members. Their interconnection, the fact that they strongly affect and influence one another, is a central part of understanding how the organization functions and how to change it.

Interconnections Among the Four Streams

The four organizational streams affect one another in significant and powerful ways. Changing one affects the others. The design of one influences the functioning of the others. Sometimes these influences and impacts are distinct and substantial; at other times the effects are difficult to identify or are relatively slight. In all cases, the connections are there and need to be understood.

Size and luxuriousness of office (PS) give off signals about the status of people which can support or contradict either or both the formal organization chart (OA) or the informal networks that evolve out of humans interacting with one another (SF). The latter two factors also have direct impacts on each other. The culture of the system (SF) strongly affects both the formulation of the organization's strategy and its implementation (OA). Organizational structures (OA) may just not work if the informal communications networks (SF) of the system are not consistent with them. The machinery used in the production process (T), the way jobs are designed (T) and performance evaluated (OA) affect the cultural norms that might evolve. Administrative policies (OA) may not be consistent with the values of the organization (SF).

Let's consider a more concrete example as a way of demonstrating the singular effects of each dimension, as well as the impact one dimension has in the context of the other three.

If two individual's jobs are reciprocally interdependent, that is, the design of the work flow (T) is such that the performance of each one's job is heavily dependent on the performance of the other's job, then the proximity of their work spaces (PS) plays an important role in the effectiveness of both. If they are separated by some distance and must communicate with each other by telephone, or must make more than a minimal effort to see each other, then the physical space design may cause a potentially severe problem. The procedure through which the persons are evaluated and the rewards associated with performance (OA) must be consistent with the interdependence of the jobs or else effective performance will be inhibited. The culture of the organization (SF) must value collaborative effort since it would support the interdependence of the jobs.

Thus, the main message is that all four dimensions of the organization are interconnected. If one is going to be changed and the effects on the others are not considered, then the impact of what is done will be reduced. It is as simple as that. Saying that is much easier than actually accomplishing it because the organizational world is so very complicated that all things cannot be controlled. If the person trying to change a system is a middle manager and cannot change some factors such as the pay system, then the person must recognize the inhibiting effect of this limitation. The person may lower his or her expectations about what is possible to accomplish while expanding options for actions to counteract the impact of those factors that cannot be changed.

Figure 3–4 depicts the interconnectedness of the four organizational streams. It also shows their relationship to the organization member.

Impact of Four Streams on Organizational Members

Let us now turn to the question of how these four organizational streams affect the behavior of individuals in the organization. Earlier, I proposed that these dimensions make up the environment for the individual and that they provide the signals about what behaviors are appropriate, desirable, and effective for the system. From a design point of view, the key strategy for changing a system is to design each of the four areas in such a way that all give the same message to people about their behavior. In terms of social cognitive theory, the messages coming from

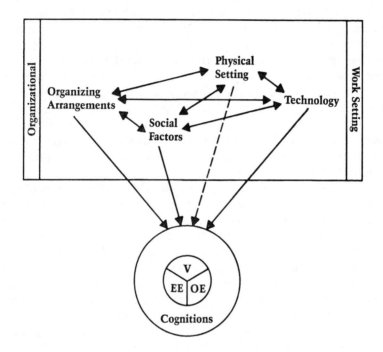

Key

V = Valence
EE = Efficacy Expectation
OE = Outcome Expectation

Figure 3–4

Components of Work Setting and Their Impact on Individual Cognitions

the work environment should affect each individual's efficacy and outcome expectations (as well as valences) in such a manner that desired new behaviors are more likely to occur.

For example, what structural design would promote greater communication? What kind of value changes would have to occur in the culture to facilitate increased openness? What kind of Physical Setting could be set up to help people bump into each other more easily? How could jobs be designed so that people would interact and exchange relevant information?

The point is to consider all four main streams at once and ask, "What can I do in each of these areas to try to deliver the message that interacting with people, communicating, and exchanging information is an important behavior that we want to have?" Asking this question often opens up different designs as well as other arenas for action. All this is driven by the fact that one is trying to get each of the four streams to deliver congruent and consistent messages about desired behaviors.

To the degree that the messages are made consistent, then more successful change will occur. It is in the situations when one area is changed and others are not or when they are changed in ways that deliver inconsistent messages, that people become confused and their response becomes difficult to predict. Some will change their behavior while others will not. Those who do change will do so in a variety of unexpected ways. Those who do not will often become even more fixed in their previous behaviors because of the anxiety caused by the risks they perceive in trying anything new.

Although the notion that mixed environmental signals should be avoided is a simple idea and not all that new, it still is very difficult to implement because there are an enormous number of variables to play with. And, as I said above, some are under an individual's control and influence and some are not.

Summary

Four streams of an organization have been identified and described. Together, they constitute the work environment for each individual. Each is a dimension composed of a series of components and each of these components sends messages to the individual about how he or she ought to behave. Since people choose behaviors based in large part on the messages they get from their environment defining the consequences of particular behaviors, it is imperative to avoid contradictions in these messages.

When contradictions occur, and they usually do, each organization member will respond to a unique pattern of these messages, perceiving some and missing others, valuing some and ignoring others, remembering some and forgetting others. As a result, predicting how any one individual will behave as a consequence of a contradictory set of messages is very difficult. More than likely, the behaviors that will occur are going to be quite mixed.

On the other hand, if relatively few contradictions exist in the message pattern sent by the four streams, then the unique mix of messages received by each member of an organization will contain a preponderance of signals telling that individual to employ a particular set of behaviors. Because every individual perceives the world differently, the exact pattern of signals received will be unique, and each person may choose to employ some behaviors not chosen by others. Nonetheless, most of the behaviors will tend to be the same ones chosen by others since the majority of messages are targeted on a common set. Although not everyone in the organization will end up behaving in exactly the same manner, relatively more people will be behaving the same if the signals they have received are not contradictory.

Now that we have established a basis for understanding the work setting each person faces in the organization, let us next consider the ways in which the four organizational streams of the work environment are determined. The focus of the next section is on these processes.

Organizational Purpose

The four streams of the organization provide an environment for each member to work in and, for maximum effectiveness, should deliver consistent and mutually reinforcing signals about desired behaviors. The four streams also are themselves influenced by the environment external to the organization. This section will describe organizational *purpose*[23] and the role it plays with respect to the definition and integration of the four key work setting dimensions. The development of this final set of concepts will lead to the presentation of a composite model of organization derived from all the ideas discussed.

Organizations exist for a variety of reasons. These reasons guide the decisions made by both the leaders and members of the system. The collective reasons for an organization's existence are called the *purpose* of the organization. This section will focus on the organization's purpose, the role it plays in helping to integrate the various parts of the organization, and the way in which it helps decision makers interpret the environment in which the organization operates.

What Is Purpose?

Very simply, the purpose of an organization is its fundamental reason for being.[24] One can arrive at a description of an organization's purpose by answering questions such as: What are we all about? Why do we exist? Why are we here? Through answers to these questions an organization can begin to understand the reasons behind why it is the way it is, or does the things it does.

From organizational design and adaptation perspectives, purpose plays two key roles. Most of the internal characteristics of the organization evolve as a reflection of its overriding purpose, and most of the organization's reaction to shifts in environmental conditions are interpreted using purpose as a guiding framework. Yet, in spite of its importance to system effectiveness, purpose remains the aspect of organizational functioning that is least clearly specified and most widely misunderstood.

Many managers of business organizations, when asked to describe the purpose of their organization, immediately respond that their purpose is to make money. When pressed further, they

---

[23]I would like to thank Warren Klein of Sandia Laboratories for his contribution to the ideas presented in this section.

[24]I have used the words *purpose* and *reason* in the singular for ease of presentation, but, in reality, the plural should be used. An organization has more than one purpose or reason for being.

tend to admit that that is not the only purpose of their organization, there are other things. Certainly, making money is a necessary condition for continued existence, but, just as certainly for most, it is not the only reason they see for existing.

So, the purpose of a business organization is more than just to make money. What else might it be? As most managers answer that question, they often find themselves becoming fairly abstract or philosophical. Some respond with reasons for existence such as, "to help the world communicate," "to give pleasure to people as they are being transported from one location to another," "to provide the energy needed for the world to prosper," or "to service the computing needs of our customers while at the same time providing opportunities for our employees to develop their abilities."

As one can see from these purpose statements, reasons for being are more abstract and fundamental than the typical mission statements or goal statements that are a central part of any good strategic planning process. The latter types grow out of purpose statements and are more operational in tone and texture.

Vision, another common concept used to guide organizations, is not the same as purpose. Vision is one way that purpose gets translated into organizational realities and is more tangible. A vision is often a representation of what the organization might look like if it were accomplishing its purpose. Vision *reflects* the core reasons for the organization's existence and, as such, is like a star out on the horizon that broadly guides decision makers as they pick and choose among the many short-term options and paths available to the organization.

Purpose provides the framework around which the organization can design itself and make decisions about the actions it wishes to take to meet its environmental challenges. Through the organization's internal characteristics and actions taken to respond to the demands placed on it, *purpose permeates the entire existence of an organization and directly or indirectly drives many of the decisions and behaviors of the organization's members.* For the individual member, purpose provides guidance, energy, focus, motivation, and a justification for being a part of the organization. Figure 3–5 depicts this dual role of organizational purpose.

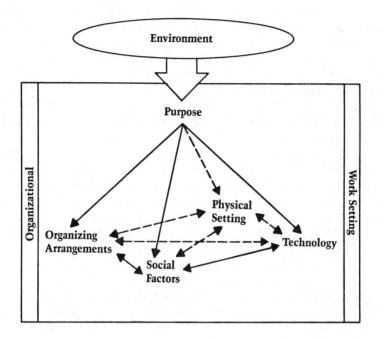

Figure 3–5
Purpose of Mediator between Environment and Work Setting

Purpose and the Four Organizational Streams

Decisions are constantly being made about how each of the four streams should look: Should we have a matrix structure? What kind of strategy should we follow? How should we deal with the conflicts we are having? Which norms could help us be more efficient? How should people's jobs be set up to create maximum motivation and development for our employees? How should the speed of the production line be regulated? Where should we put a particular group's offices? Should we move to an open office environment?

These decisions affect what the work setting is like, what messages it delivers to its members, and, consequently, how they will behave on the job. Yet, often different people in the organization are responsible for making decisions in each of these realms. In a manufacturing plant, the plant manager makes decisions that establish the design of people's jobs, the personnel manager decides on the pay scheme for plant employees, the facilities manager chooses the architectural design for the plant, the group vice president decides what values the organization should have, the accounting manager designs the cost control system, the training manager develops the training for problem-solving, and so on.

Each of these actors is, in effect, determining a part of the overall organization. If they do not hold a common view of its purpose, many will make decisions, about the particular set of factors they influence, guided by unknown criteria. It is likely that the personal purpose of the individual decision makers, along with their own vague views or interpretations of the overall organization's purpose, will guide the decision-making process. If the organization's purpose is not clear in each person's mind, then their own purpose will most likely take precedence and their respective decisions will be mainly based on that.

Since every decision maker is a unique person, with a different set of individual purposes, the decisions made by each most likely will not be highly congruent with the decisions of others. To the degree that they are not, many parts of the organization will wind up working at cross purposes. So, for example, the manufacturing manager's personal purpose may be the creation of a maximally efficient department and so that manager may design jobs that are highly specialized and easy to control. The personnel manager may design a reward system that does not focus on quality of output but instead is based on seniority. The facilities manager may select a design that provides a bright, airy feeling in the plant and that allows people easy access to each other.

The decisions of each of the managers in this short set of examples, are, to a greater or lesser degree, inconsistent with those of the others. A highly specialized job combined with seniority-based pay and located in a setting that facilitates talking to others may not lead to employees producing large quantities of high-quality products in minimal time. More than likely, the outcome will be people bored with highly specialized jobs who feel resentful of the excessive control, who don't feel motivated to produce high volumes of output, who spend lots of time on non-work-related talk with co-workers, and who, more than likely, will frequently be late or absent and relatively unproductive.

We can see that, ideally, a clearly understood and broadly accepted purpose serves the function of integrating the four main streams of the organization. It is the glue that holds everything together and keeps the parts moving in concert. It guides those decisions that affect the design of the organization and it provides a direction and focus for the individual employee interested in helping the organization become more successful. Hence, its importance cannot be underestimated.

Yet, the harsh reality is that few organizations possess a clearly articulated, widely disseminated, and broadly supported organizational purpose. In most cases, the organization has, at best, specified a mission statement describing something along the lines of producing quality products, at low cost, to serve the needs of the marketplace, with the end of creating added wealth for the stockholder. These statements do not really tell everyone in the organization exactly what the organization's reason for existence is, what it is all about, and why it is there. If they did, and, if people in the system subscribed to them, then one could expect that, as people went about doing their jobs in the organization, they would be guided by these principles and would be more likely to make decisions consistent with them than if the clearly stated purpose did not exist.

Purpose and the Organization's Environment

Not only does the purpose of the organization have an effect inward, into the organization, but it also plays a role outward, into the external environment of the system. It provides a means for interpreting the environment in organizational terms. In this capacity, it acts as a lens or filter through which environmental events may be seen and then translated into internal action. Managers, using the organization's purpose as their guiding framework, decide on responses to environmental changes. The same environmental changes may trigger quite different organizational adaptations if the organizations in question possess radically different purposes.

Recent events in the electronics industry have provided some sharply contrasting examples. The downturn in microchip demand triggered quite varied responses from several organizations. One announced that it was substantially increasing its investment in research and development while another, in the face of the same environmental conditions, announced the exact opposite reaction, a significant reduction in R&D expenditures. How does one explain these opposite responses?

There are a variety of factors that might come into play. The perspective we are developing here points to the purposes of the two organizations and how they differ. The first organization's purpose emphasizes leadership in innovation, a challenging environment for employees, and contribution to customers by providing them with state-of-the-art products. The second focuses on the organization's responsibility to provide high returns to investors at acceptable levels of risk, to produce high-quality products at minimal cost, and to provide a just and honest working environment for its employees.

Analysis of these two organizational purposes reveals how the same environmental shift led to different responses by the two systems. The first sees, as one of its main reasons for being, the creation of products at technology's cutting edge. It saw a downturn in market demand as an opportunity to turn more of its efforts to this creative task so that, in the long term, it would be ready with the very latest products when the market improved. In contrast, the second organization did not see itself as the innovation leader. Rather, it saw itself as providing returns to stockholders and protecting their investment in the corporation. It wanted to maintain quality while minimizing costs, thus maximizing short-term returns. In a market downturn, the second organization believed it perfectly reasonable to cut costs in whatever ways possible, and a decrease in R&D spending was certainly a place to make substantial reductions in expenditures.

A second example of how organizational purpose provides the lenses for interpreting environmental shifts occurred in the computer industry. The dip in personal computer sales forced all companies in that field to curtail costs severely. Two very similar computer companies responded quite differently to the cost reduction challenge. It was clear to both companies that employee costs had to somehow be reduced. One laid off 10% of its work force for an indefinite period of time. The second reduced its work month by 10%; that is, all employees were given one day off without pay every two weeks. The main difference in the purpose statements of the two companies was that the second strongly emphasized the importance of its human resources while the first did not even mention them. Instead, it focused on its responsibility to protect and increase the stockholders' equity and return on investment.

These two examples show that organizations live in rapidly changing environments and, in order to remain viable, must respond to sudden shifts. The way organizations interpret changes in their environments is, no doubt, driven by numerous factors. One dominant factor is the purpose of the organization. It provides a basis from which organizational leaders can interpret the meaning of environmental shifts for their organizations. Different purposes will drive managers to focus on different aspects of an environmental shift or to conclude that different actions are appropriate ways of "living the purpose" they see for their organizations.

Therefore, when attempting to understand why an organization behaved the way it did in response to changing environmental demands, one must look at its purpose. If the organization's purpose is clear and widely supported, it should be relatively easy to understand why it did what it did. If, on the other hand, the organizational purpose is not clear, then one must assess the purposes of the key individuals involved in deciding the course of the organization's response to environmental change. Their decision making was driven by what they saw as the organization's purpose as well as by their own personal purpose. Admittedly, in the case of a clear organizational purpose, the decision makers' personal purposes also come into play. I would propose, however, that they have a much less significant effect than in the second case.

In summary, the organization's purpose plays two central roles. One, directed inward, serves to coordinate the design of each major organizational stream. The second, directed outward, provides a basis for organizational interpretations of environmental shifts and the consequent channeling of organizational response.

Integrating the Pieces

We now have all the pieces necessary to present a more complete model of organizations, one that can be used as a basis for understanding how to change a system. My main intention in developing it has been twofold. First, I believe that all successful managers and change consultants do their work based on a model of how an organization works. They carry it around in their heads. Usually it is not clearly verbalized and gets used intuitively instead of analytically. One common consequence is that the person is not consistent in using the model held or forgets critical parts of it at inopportune times. As a result, planned organizational change efforts wind up evolving in somewhat erratic ways and often fail. I believe it important to make my view of organizations clear in the hope that it will motivate others to clarify their views.

The second major reason for presenting this model is that it provides a conceptual basis for both the Stream Analysis approach in general and the structure of the Stream Charts specifically. More concretely, the model provides a basis for understanding why organizational members are behaving in dysfunctional ways and can guide the selection of interventions designed to alter their behaviors.

Figure 3–6 consolidates the various ideas presented thus far. It begins with the environment's impact on the organizational work setting through the purpose of the system. The purpose guides the design of each of four central organizational dimensions. These dimensions, or streams, constitute the work setting for the individual, who looks to it for cues about the behaviors that will most likely get him or her what he or she wants from being in the organization. Based on the cues received, the people's expectations or values are altered and they choose on-the-job behaviors that either increase or decrease the overall performance of the organization as well as their own individual psychological development. Both on-the-job behavior and organizational performance affect the characteristics of the work setting, the latter factor also having an impact on the external environment of the system. The external environment affects organizational members directly but usually outside the confines of the organizational situation.

The model shown in the figure is intended to be sufficiently complex so as to capture the most important aspects of organizational life while not so detailed that it engenders confusion. So many things happen in an organization that without some sort of organizing principle it is virtually impossible to understand what is going on. It is hoped that the Stream Organization Model will help prevent some of the misdiagnoses of ills in organizational processes that lead to incorrect change interventions, perhaps the most common cause of failures in planned change. It is for this reason too that this chapter has emphasized so strongly the conceptual roots of Stream Analysis.

The Stream Organization Model in Context

Before closing it is appropriate to compare the Stream Organization Model with those proposed by other authors of Addison-Wesley OD Series books, most notably Kotter,[25] Gal-

---

[25]J. P. Kotter, *Organizational Dynamics: Diagnosis and Intervention* (Reading, Mass.: Addison-Wesley, 1978).

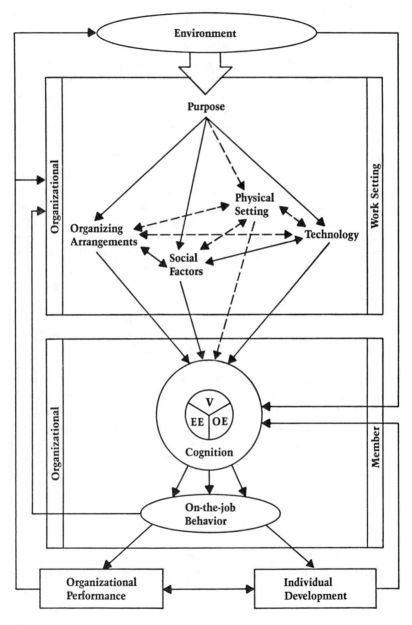

Figure 3–6
Stream Organization Model

braith,[26] and Beckhard and Harris[27] in addition to ones developed by Beer,[28] Nadler,[29] and Weisbord.[30] Of these six models, five (Beckhard and Harris, Beer, Kotter, Nadler, and Weisbord) were based on systems theory, as is the Stream Organization Model. The sixth, Galbraith, begins with different assumptions about a fundamental organizational paradigm. He roots his arguments in contingency theory and the relationship between task uncertainty and information requirements. Of the models based on systems theory, the Beer, Kotter, Nadler, and Weisbord models are most clearly structured in terms of defining a broad range of organizational variables and in specifying the relationships among them. For this reason, I will focus my discussion on these four models.

A comparison of the Stream Organization Model (SOM) with the four other models shows that all the key variables in each of the four are accounted for in the SOM. The same is not true of the reverse comparison. Physical setting, as an important organizational variable, is not mentioned by any of the four models. Purpose of the organization is mentioned specifically only by Weisbord. The technology of the organization is not a part of either the Beer or the Weisbord models and only its task component is considered by Nadler. Furthermore, from the perspective of parsimony, the SOM describes the fundamental transformation process in four broad variable sets. Nadler also uses only four but omits the physical setting and, as noted above, considers only task rather than the broader concept of organizational technology. The other models use five to eight variable sets to define the same transformation function, while, again, omitting Physical Setting.

Both Beer and Nadler depict the organization as a process flowing from inputs through transformation to outputs, as does

[26]J. Galbraith, *Designing Complex Organizations* (Reading, Mass.: Addison-Wesley, 1973).

[27]R. Beckhard and R. T. Harris, *Organizational Transitions: Managing Complex Change*, 2nd ed. (Reading, Mass.: Addison-Wesley, 1987).

[28]M. Beer, *Organization Change and Development: A Systems View* (Santa Monica, Calif.: Goodyear, 1980).

[29]D. A. Nadler, Managing organizational change: an integrative perspective. *Journal of Applied Behavioral Science*, vol. 17 (1981):191–211.

[30]Weisbord, *Organizational Diagnosis*.

the SOM. Kotter and Weisbord, on the other hand, represent the organization in such a manner that a process flow cannot be discerned. This makes it more difficult to understand the specific context in which organizational malfunctionings are occurring and the variables most closely associated with any difficulties identified.

Finally, none of the other models places the behavior of individuals as the key mediating factor in organizational change. The SOM is clearly based on understanding the conditions that lead to behavioral change because those conditions are the leverage points for change. They are the targets of planned change interventions, because if they can be changed they will, through consequent alterations in individual behavior, change the organization's outcomes. Kotter emphasizes the "Key Organizational Processes" as the central mediating variable for change, while Weisbord focuses on leadership. Beer and Nadler do not develop a similar set of notions about their view of the world.

In terms of what might be missing in the SOM that other models might have included in their frameworks, the SOM does not emphasize strongly the financial or economic view of an organization. Although financial controls are part of the administrative systems (Organizing Arrangements stream), factors such as the value of the tangible assets of the organization (Kotter) are not clearly highlighted in the SOM. The SOM also does not prescribe a "best way" for an organization to be designed. Rather, it merely specifies the key areas for consideration and emphasizes that they should be designed so as to deliver consistent messages about desired behaviors.

The Stream Organization Model has guided change efforts in a variety of organizations ranging from service organizations such as a hospital, an electric utility, a telephone company, a community volunteer organization, and a research foundation to manufacturing companies such as a high-technology firm, an aerospace firm, and a construction organization. In all of these settings, I have found it useful for structuring my view of the complexity of organizational life.

With the Stream Organization Model as a background, I would like now to turn to a detailed description of three applications of Stream Analysis. All three examples use the SOM as the basis for establishing the contents of each organizational category in the Stream Charts. As such, they will demonstrate the application of the SOM to organizational diagnosis and change planning.

4

Applications of Stream Analysis

This chapter will describe three different applications of Stream Analysis.[1] The first occurred in an organization experiencing difficulties in a particular aspect of its functioning. The problem had been identified and the organization wanted to focus change efforts around its resolution. The second describes a situation in which a major change had already been decided on; a diagnosis and plan were needed to determine what actions to take and how to implement them. The third describes a broad-based diagnosis of an organization wanting to examine thoroughly all aspects of its functioning as the first step in a comprehensive change effort.

In the first example, each of the three major uses of Stream Analysis (diagnosing, planning, and tracking change) occurred. In the second, only the diagnosis and an abbreviated form of plan-

---

[1]Portions of this chapter are drawn from J. I. Porras and J. Harkness, "Managing Planned Change: A Stream Approach." In R. Tannenbaum, N. Margulies, F. Massarik and Associates, *Human Systems Development* (San Francisco: Jossey-Bass, 1985), pp. 224–245, and from J. Harkness, Case Study in Stream Analysis, unpublished manuscript, 1986.

ning were used. In the third, the stream charting technique was used in the diagnostic process only. In all three cases, the steps followed and the charts developed are presented to give the reader a detailed view of how the technique was applied.

Dealing with a Particular Problem Area

A large community hospital had been experiencing explosive growth for six years, with the operating room department (OR) bearing most of the brunt of the changes that had ensued. Surgical procedures rose during that period from approximately 6,000 per year to more than 10,000 per year. The ever increasing demand for additional operating room space necessitated a protracted and complex renovation and expansion of the physical facilities, both in and surrounding the OR itself. Overall OR floorspace tripled as the number of operating rooms increased from ten to fourteen and outpatient areas doubled. Facilities supporting the main OR activities, such as supply, instrument storage, and office areas, were also substantially expanded and modernized. Numerous technological innovations, driven by the influx of new surgical tools and equipment, were implemented. Finally, to handle the expanded requirements and increase in number of OR staff, a new organizational structure was designed and put in place with the help of a variety of activities, including team development, individualized counseling, process consultation, and role clarification.

Approximately three years after the organization had begun the massive development, the OR manager became familiar with the Stream Analysis technique and decided to use it on a particularly intractable problem that had been plaguing the OR for quite a long time. The project described here centers around this problem and how Stream Analysis was applied to its resolution. For simplicity of explanation and to give greater clarity on the workings of a complete Stream Analysis cycle (diagnosis, planning, and tracking), I have chosen a narrower focus for this initial discussion. Later sections will deal with broader, more complex, and less clearly defined problem situations.

The Problem Situation

By the third year of the planned change process, the OR was in the final stages of reconstructing its physical facilities. Four additional operating rooms were being planned along with a new area called the *center core* which was to contain a highly sophisticated instrument processing and supply distribution facility. Changes in other dimensions of the organization — new procedures, supply systems, instrument washing technologies, and scheduling systems — were also anticipated or in their early stages of implementation.

One component of the center core operations was not performing well, however. A group of nonprofessional employees called nursing assistants (NAs) was a constant source of difficulty for OR management. Absenteeism and turnover in this group were the highest of any OR group, while their job performance was perceived to be the lowest.

The NAs' job functions were to transport patients to and from the OR, run errands, handle supplies, wash instruments, and respond to spur-of-the-moment requests from the professional staff. Although these were their formally assigned functions, most of what the NAs did was relatively undefined. As a result, managing them effectively had eluded the formal structure of the OR and seemed an unsolvable problem.

A sudden and very substantial increase in workload highlighted the need to change the NAs' role and to develop the proper conditions to support their new responsibilities. The OR director believed that effective management of NAs was now paramount and decided to use Stream Analysis as a way of developing a clearer view of the problems and their roots. Following are the steps she took and the results of her efforts.

Stream Analysis

1. Formation of a Change Management Team (CMT). The first thing the OR director did was to create a change management team. Since time was of the essence and the director did not want to consume more of it training a larger group in the stream method, she decided to call upon only the materials management coordinator (MMC) to participate with her in the diagnostic and planning processes. The MMC had worked closely with NAs for a number of years and had experienced all of the operating difficulties first hand. So, together, the OR director and the materials management coordinator made up the change management team.

2. Information Collection. The OR director and the MMC met and listed all the problems they had encountered in working with and trying to manage NAs over the previous few months. Their review and discussion yielded the following observations.

The NA job was an entry level position, paying relatively low wages, requiring no basic skills, affording no opportunity for advancement, and receiving minimal status in the organization. Formally, the NA group was located at the very bottom of the organization, reporting directly to almost everyone in the OR and, therefore, in effect, responsible to no one. No written policies or procedures governing NAs' work existed, making it quite difficult to assess either their performance or reliability. The lack of formal job definitions further exacerbated this difficulty.

A variety of immediate problems had surfaced which were making the situation even more critical. Conflict had arisen between NAs and the nursing staff. A new case cart system had been started in which all of the supplies needed for a given surgical case were preloaded into a cart and placed in the appropriate operating room immediately before the scheduled surgery time. The NAs were responsible for moving the loaded case cart from the supply area to the operating room. This was an important shift of responsibility from the nurses to the NAs. This new system was creating two sets of problems.

The first was a conflict that it created with the performance of another important NA task, patient transport. Changing to a case cart system meant that the nurses would no longer be gathering all the supplies needed for all their cases onto one table prior to the start of the daily schedule each morning. The NAs would soon be responsible for bringing the supplies into the operating room just prior to each case, while at the same time transporting the patient. The timing in the flow of patients and supplies through an operating room is critical. Since the number of operations was increasing to approximately sixty per day, with seven or eight rooms having to be readied for the next operation at once, performing these two tasks simultaneously would require almost double the present number of NAs sporadically through the day.

The second major problem was a conflict of another type — one between the nurses and the NAs. The nurses were chastising the NAs for not being available when they needed them to get supplies. The new case cart system was aggravating this conflict because, often, in preparation for a surgical procedure, the nurses would open the case carts to find that not all needed supplies were there. This would cause a delay until the missing supplies could be brought in by the NAs from the OR supply room. This was not only placing increased demands on the NAs' time, it was also requiring them to be more immediately available to prevent delays during the surgical procedure. As far as the nurses were concerned, the NAs were now making themselves less available when the need for their services was even more urgent. In fact, instead of working harder, it seemed to the nurses that the NAs were always "gabbing" someplace rather than working. The NAs, in turn, did not feel they should be held responsible for correcting mistakes made by the Central Supply employees who were supposed to make sure all supplies were on the case cart.

The NAs were quite frustrated and felt that they were being picked on by everybody. The MMC reported a conversation she had had that day with one of the rare NAs who had been in the OR for over five years.

> The instrument washer is on the blink again, [he had told the MMC]. This is the third time this week. How can I get the instruments clean when the washer doesn't work and there aren't enough people to do them by hand? It's 9:00 A.M., our busiest time with five ORs finishing at once and dirty instruments piling up. No one's around to help because they're all up on the wards getting those next five patients. Thirty minutes from now they'll all be standing around with nothing to do. In the meantime, the nurses are calling for instruments and I can't deliver! It's the same old story over and over again. They don't pay me enough

to take this abuse. No one appreciates what I go through to keep these instruments moving. None of us NAs ever gets any thanks for all we do.

The OR director countered with a story of her own that had occurred the previous morning. An NA came to the OR director's office to complain about having been chewed out by the nurse in Number 3 OR because the scrub solution wasn't mixed right. The NA wondered how she was supposed to know how to do it right since there was no written procedure on how to do it. She said that she had been taught how to do it by another NA, but apparently the procedure she had learned was wrong.

The discussion between the OR director and the MMC ended with several observations: the NAs had no assigned area where they might be found if they were not accomplishing one of their assigned tasks; there was no way to reach the NAs by telephone or intercom; and finally there was no way to formally evaluate their performance since they reported to no one special person or had clearly defined duties, or could be observed in the performance of those duties.

3. Classification of Problems into Streams. The next step in Stream Analysis is to reach a consensus over the meaning of each problem and to classify it into a particular stream.[2] In the OR case, the director and the MMC thoroughly discussed each problem and jointly decided on its classification. They then created a Stream Chart on a large sheet of newsprint and placed each problem in its appropriate stream.

It should be noted that this process took four to five hours because, often, there were conflicting views of what each problem was all about. In attempting to classify a problem into a stream, the two managers found themselves having quite different views

---

[2]Ralph Killman's work on assumptional analysis is relevant here. In deciding which stream to classify each problem as, differences in perspective come into play. Not only do people differ in the ways they view the meaning of each problem (a marketing manager may see a particular problem quite differently than a manufacturing manager), but they also differ on the assumptions they hold about how things should be (a particular situation reflects the way things should be for the marketing manager while the manufacturing manager believes that the situation is totally wrong).

of what the problem actually was. The classification process highlighted these differing views and led to substantially improved understandings on the part of both managers.

4. Establishing Interconnections among Problems. After the problems have been classified, an analysis is conducted to determine how they are interconnected. In this case, the two managers systematically focused on each problem and asked themselves and each other, "Is this problem driving any of the other problems we have identified? Are any of the other problems driving this problem?" Sometimes the answer to each of these questions would be quite clear. At other times, they could not convincingly argue what the causal direction was, but only that the two problems were related. In these cases, two causal arrows would be drawn, one pointing in either direction.[3]

Once again, increased understanding and a shared view of the problems were key outcomes of this process. The latter result, a shared view, is perhaps the most important consequence of this process. Corrective action is most effective, all other things equal, when everyone involved in taking action share a common understanding of the problem situation. Many change efforts have gone astray because the different actors responsible for solving the organization's problems don't all see the situation in the same way.

The Diagnostic Stream Chart that resulted from steps 3 and 4 is shown in Fig. 4–1. It is important to note that this chart is a snapshot of the organization at one point in time. But as a snapshot, it is not oriented to reflect situations that are transient and that occurred only at the time the stream picture was taken. Rather, the snapshot reflects the cumulative state of affairs up to that moment. As such, it shows those issues which are persisting and which will not go away unless they are dealt with in some concerted manner.

---

[3]Later on we discovered that this was not a good technique. It became important to force a decision about the direction of the arrow; it had to go in one direction or the other but not both. The analysis of interconnections is clearer if the arrows are not two-headed. Within every case we have worked, participants in the process have been able to push their thinking to the point that they have been able to make a decision to have the arrow point one way or the other.

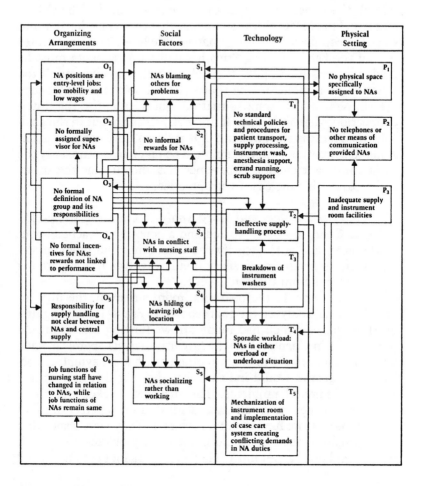

Figure 4–1
Stream Diagnostic Chart

The stream diagram shown in the figure also does not contain all the issues existing at the time it was made. The OR director and the MMC eliminated those that they considered minor so as to keep the analysis at a manageable level. This constitutes part of the "art" of using Stream Analysis. Judgments must be made by users to simplify their charts when appropriate. If too much detail is included, the charts become so complex that they are unusable. The same situation holds true for the interconnections that are drawn. If too many lines are put in the analysis, the result is so confusing that it doesn't help one to understand the situation better. Care must be taken to capture only the most important events. Experience has shown that the users' ability to do this increases with practice.

5. *Core Problem and Story Analysis.* Once the Stream Diagnostic Chart has been created and a consensus reached about it, the next step is to identify the core issues and problem stories. Performing this analysis normally involves first separating the symptoms from the core issues.

Symptoms. In the operating room situation, the director and the MMC analyzed the chart shown in Fig. 4–1, focusing first on those boxes which had many arrows flowing into them. As pointed out in Chapter 2, in the Stream Analysis approach, such boxes are more likely to contain problems that are symptoms because the arrows would indicate that they are driven by other, more fundamental problems. The managers picked out those boxes which they then validated, with their own perceptions, as symptoms of more fundamental problems. They were issues that most people in the OR would point to as problems and which were complained about most. They received a lot of attention and energy.

In fact, these problems had been identified before and efforts had been made to resolve them. However, the previous efforts had not made these problems go away. This latter observation by the two managers gave further credibility to the validity of the chart analysis which indicated that these problems were symptoms rather than fundamental problems.

The two most obvious examples of symptoms occurred in the Social Factors stream, items S_3 (NA conflict with nursing staff) and S_4 (NAs hiding or leaving job location). Both of these problems had disturbed the director and MMC for several months, but, as noted above, all their efforts to solve them had not yielded any positive results.

The Stream Diagnostic Chart gives some insight as to why these problems didn't stay solved when various actions were taken. For example, as reported earlier, since there were no formal definitions of NA responsibilities, the nurses expected the NAs to perform certain tasks while the NAs did not think those tasks were part of their responsibilities. No clear way existed of resolving this disagreement without some formally defined set of NA responsibilities. Until responsibilities became clearly defined, there would always be new situations cropping up which would trigger NA–nurse conflict. The ineffective supply handling process and breakdown of instrument washing equipment also added opportunities for the two groups to come into conflict.

A similar set of arguments can be made to explain why the NAs hid or left their job location. It was another way of responding to the same sets of pressures that were causing conflict with the nurses.

This situation is a typical example of how Stream Analysis drives one to a deeper analysis of a situation. Common diagnostic approaches would have identified the NA–nurse conflict as an extremely pressing problem and would have then triggered interventions designed to deal with those conflicts. Intergroup conflict resolution techniques might have been applied to reducing the conflict between the two groups.

In the use of these techniques, perhaps the more fundamental problems noted above may have surfaced and actions taken to resolve them. On the other hand, they may not have been readily identified and the time necessary to understand the roots of the conflict substantially increased.

Using Stream Analysis, one would be driven to take care of the more fundamental sources of the conflict before trying to deal directly with the conflicting parties. It could be that correcting the driving problems might eliminate the conflict altogether, thus saving the energy necessary to bring the two groups together for conflict resolution. If not, then more than likely the conflict would be at a much lower level once the driving forces had been removed, and therefore it would be much more manageable.

Core Problems. Identification of the core problems begins by picking out those boxes that have many arrows coming out of them. These are the issues that contribute to the existence of those other problems which are usually, but not always, symptoms.[4] Problem O_3, "No formal definition of NA group and its responsibilities," is the most obvious issue in this category. It has numerous arrows coming out of it, so it plays a central role in driving other problems. This would classify it as a key problem, one that needs to be attacked early in any planned change process.

A second core problem shows up in the Physical Setting stream, P_3, "Inadequate supply and instrument room facilities." It drives four other problems, one in the Physical Setting stream (P_2), two in the Technology stream (T_2 and T_4), and one in the Social Factors stream (S_5). Although not as powerful a core problem as O_3, it nevertheless was seen by the OR manager and the MMC as a critical one to attack early on in any change process.

A third core problem, not made as obvious by the number of arrows coming out of it as O_3 and P_3, is T_5, "Mechanization of instrument room and implementation of case-cart system creating conflicting demands in NA duties." Although the chart does not easily point to this problem as a core problem, it is a good example of how the greater knowledge of the organization that resides in the heads of the people using the Stream technique comes into play. Until the analysis, there had been enough slack in the system that the conflicting demands for the NAs, as noted earlier, to be at two places at once, could be dealt with. However, the OR managers knew that the increasing demands for surgical procedures would make it impossible to continue this practice in

---

[4]At this stage in the development of the Stream Analysis technique the identification of core problems is based on a rather simplistic algorithm — frequency counts and clinical judgments of the change process leaders. More sophisticated statistical techniques that could involve the use of weighting schemes to represent the importance of each interconnecting arrow are certainly possible. In that regard, existing approaches to identifying core problems such as triangulation, regressing outcome measures on measures of antecedent variables, using a priori theoretical frameworks, and so forth could provide insights for more sophisticated approaches to identifying core problems using the Stream Approach.

the future. The problem, therefore, was much more critical than indicated by the mechanics of the analysis.

The key message in this example is that the technique of Stream Analysis does not replace the vast knowledge and experience of its users. It is designed to augment and systematize the thinking of an organization's members. It should not be used in such a manner that it bypasses the intuitions and opinions of the people using it. Instead, it should blend in with their hunches, challenge their biases, and result in a more integrated and richer view of the organization's problems than could be achieved by using either the manager's perceptions or the Stream Charts alone.

A second type of core problem exists, one more subtle and difficult to tease out in any diagnostic process. It shows up in a Stream Chart as a problem that drives core problems such as O_3 but which, at the same time, tends not to be driven by anything else. T_1, "No standard technical policies and procedures for . . . ," is an example of this type of problem. It drives O_3, but, is not driven by anything else.

Called a fundamental core problem, this type of problem often goes undetected using normal diagnostic approaches. Yet, it is solving just this type of problem that gives the greatest leverage on the largest number of additional problems. Dealing with it does not necessarily make the other problems disappear completely, but it does alleviate them and make them much more tractable. For this reason, fundamental core problems are the "nuggets" in Stream Analysis.

In summary, then, this stage in analyzing the Stream Diagnostic Chart yielded one fundamental core problem and three, more intermediate, core problems. The former was the lack of standard technical policies and procedures (T_1), and the latter were the absence of a formal definition of the NA group and its responsibilities (O_3); conflicting demands in NA duties (T_5); and inadequate supply and instrument room facilities (P_3). Identification of core problems leads then to the final stage in analysis of the diagnostic chart — identification of problem stories.

Critical Problem Stories. Critical problem stories are strings of problems that, when taken together, create a broader, more global issue. For example, "a firefighting mentality" in an organization is a more global problem that can consist of a series of problems all linked together in a causal chain. Conceptualizing the issue at a broader level can help keep people on target when implementing solutions to the various component parts of the larger, more complex issue. This is the benefit of identifying these more comprehensive problem stories.

In the OR situation, an example story is shown in Fig. 4–2. This story can be characterized by the dysfunctional norms and interaction processes that had developed in the culture of the organization. Blaming, socializing, conflicting, hiding had all become part of the social fabric of organizational life for the NAs. These behavioral patterns were driven in part by each other (that is, they fed each other), and in part by the sporadic workload. The workload sometimes made unrealistic demands on the NA, while at other times, by not providing any demand, it facilitated the NA looking for mental stimulation elsewhere.

The sporadic workload is driven mainly by the three core problems identified earlier: an absence of formal NA structure (O_3), conflicting demands on NAs (T_5), and inadequate facilities (P_3). The combination of organizational structure, job design, and physical facilities both provide the basis for understanding the forces driving the sporadic workload process and point to avenues for solution.

Finally, resting closer to the core of the situation is the lack of standard technical policies and procedures to provide the parameters within which the structural position of the NA group could be designed.

As a collection of interconnected problems, this story of issues provides a richer view of the situation and more guidance on how to go about attacking each problem independently as well as in connection with every other problem in the broader story. Through identification of stories in the Stream Diagnostic Chart, the OR director and the MMC were able to get a more comprehensive view of the problems they were facing, which led them to create more effective plans to guide the actual change process.

The Stream Chart also provided another way for the OR director and MMC to think about stories in the data. In this approach, the two managers focused on trends or tendencies in the chart as a whole. For example, in Fig. 4–1 most of the arrows

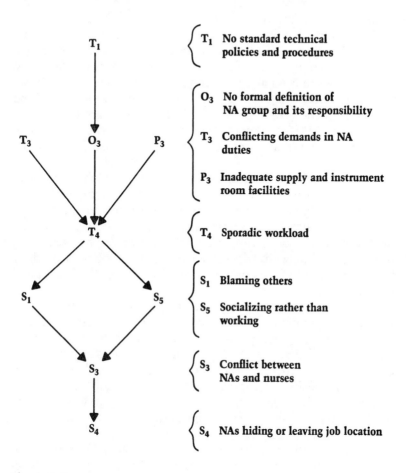

T_1 No standard technical policies and procedures

O_3 No formal definition of NA group and its responsibility

T_3 Conflicting demands in NA duties

P_3 Inadequate supply and instrument room facilities

T_4 Sporadic workload

S_1 Blaming others

S_5 Socializing rather than working

S_3 Conflict between NAs and nurses

S_4 NAs hiding or leaving job location

Figure 4–2
Example of a Problem Story

shown flow into the Social Factors stream from the other three streams. For the OR, this observation validated the director's and MMC's beliefs that a variety of deeper problems in organizational functioning were manifesting themselves in the human arena. This was in sharp contrast to the views of the nursing staff, who were seeing the NAs as the main problem and were strongly advocating actions that would deal directly with the attitudes and behaviors of the NAs. The Stream Diagnostic Chart allowed the director and MMC to demonstrate the root causes of the human problems rather than continue making easy scapegoats of the NAs.

A second observation that came out of a global review of the chart was that most of the arrows going into the Social Factors stream originated in the Organizing Arrangements stream. This implied that, for this organization at this point in time, the human problems were most directly being driven by organizing issues. Action to begin to resolve the human problems would, by necessity, have to focus on doing something about this area as a whole.

A third insight related to the origins of the Organizing Arrangements problems. The Technology stream seemed to be driving many of the problems in the OA arena. Technological problems were highlighting the deficiencies in various aspects of the organization's structure. Had the technology problems not existed, perhaps the organizing problems would not have been so pressing. However, given the fact that Technology was a source of difficulty, weaknesses that might otherwise have been inconsequential became critical.

Finally, there appeared to exist a considerable number of intrastream interconnections in both the Technology and Physical Setting streams. Problems in these areas tended to be the root causes of other problems in the same areas. On a more global level, this implied to the director and MMC that the organization contained important weaknesses in its ability to manage its technology and to provide the physical settings needed to effectively accomplish its purpose. Somehow, these weaknesses would need to be taken care of in any long-term change process.

6. *Creating an Action Plan.* The next step in the process was for the director and MMC to develop plans for action. Planned organizational change is an organic process, therefore planning more than a few months into the future should be avoided. Although every effort must be made to identify as many actions as possible, users of Stream Analysis should limit their expectations about being able to complete them all as planned. Figure 4–3 shows the initial plans developed by the director and MMC, plans based on solving the major problems identified in the diagnosis.

Note that although this chart looks similar to the one presented in Fig. 4–1, it has some critical differences. First of all, a time dimension is included to show the expected beginning and ending points for each planned change activity. Second, the lines connecting activity boxes do not imply that one activity causes another but rather that one event triggers another, or makes it possible for a subsequent event to take place. Those readers who have worked with PERT charts will recognize the similarity between it and this approach. The one substantial difference is the way stream planning lays out actions in terms of the particular organizational characteristics that will be most affected. Organizing actions into streams allows users to map them better into the diagnostic charts developed in the earlier steps of this approach. With these background ideas in mind, let us now turn back to our example and see how a planning chart was developed for the OR.

The OR director and MMC decided first to deal with two key issues: conflicting demands on the NAs (T_5) and its consequent problem, uneven workload (T_4). In order to solve these two problems concurrently, the two managers developed a broad design for a new patient holding room. This room would provide a quiet environment in the immediate vicinity of the OR, could accommodate six to eight patients, and would allow the NAs to transport patients well in advance of case preparation time. This would make the NAs available for exchanging case carts and assisting nurses in changing over an operating room from one case to the next.

Further analysis revealed an underutilization of housekeeping personnel whenever they worked within the OR. Janitors (or porters, as they were formally titled) spent only 30% of their time performing two major functions — mopping floors and carrying out soiled laundry between cases. Assumption of respon-

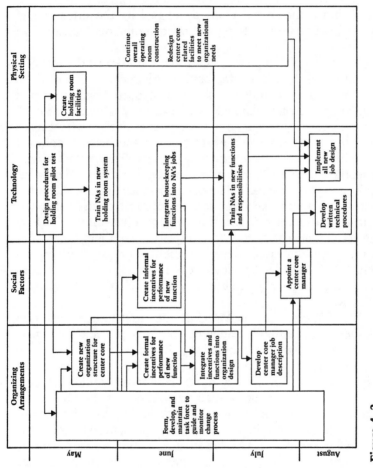

Figure 4–3
Stream Planning Chart

104

sibility for these functions by the NAs would consolidate the two roles (porter and NA) into one and eliminate significant labor hours. Furthermore, the major janitorial tasks would help fill up those times of low activity and even out the workload for the NA.

The OR director and MMC felt that since any changes to be implemented would require attention to all four streams, it would be advisable to form a task force representing expertise in each stream. Such a task force could create an organizational design for the center core that would address the needs across each stream. The two managers therefore decided to select a task force that would consist of the OR director (who represented both the Organizing Arrangements and Social Factors streams and was the final decision maker); a head nurse and the MMC (both provided expertise in the Technology and Organizing Arrangements streams); the construction coordinator (who was responsible for monitoring the ongoing reconstruction project and therefore represented the Physical Setting stream); and the staff development coordinator (who provided input and support for training and skill development in the Technology stream). In addition, since the change effort would involve three other departments as well — housekeeping, personnel, and management engineering — these managers were also requested to take part in planning the implementation process.

It was further planned that the task force would first work on its own effectiveness before trying to generate any concrete action. Once this was done, effort would be focused on developing a design for the new organization to deal with the demands for additional service and the need for a managerial framework for center core activities. A major part of this effort would be to bring action in all four streams to bear on integrating the NAs into the organizational structure in a way meaningful to them as well as effective in the overall scheme of things.

A brief description of how the actions planned were represented on the planning chart may help the reader better understand how the planning process unfolds. Since the task force would have as one of its goals the creation of a new organizational structure, this is shown in the Stream Planning Chart (Fig. 4–3) by drawing a line from the box describing the task force activity in the Social Factors stream to the one describing the creation of the new organizational structure in the Organizing Arrangements stream. In the Technology stream, the development of the holding room would trigger both the technical training of the NAs and the creation of holding room facilities. Both of these interventions are shown as being triggered by the new holding room concept.

In general, then, the planning process takes place by recognizing interconnections between boxes in the diagnostic chart and planning interventions that will deal with both the problem identified in the box and the need implied in the interconnection. Furthermore, it must be recognized that actions often trigger the need for other actions not anticipated or implied by the problem diagnosis.

7. *Implementation.* Formation of the task force occurred immediately upon conclusion of the initial planning process by the director and MMC. The Stream Analysis done up to this point was shared with the task force. Laying out the current situation in streams provided a useful introduction to both the technique of Stream Analysis and the dynamics of the problems being faced in the OR. Discussion and analysis of the diagnostic chart along with the planning chart provided direction and focus for the task force. The consequence of this was that the task force moved along very quickly. Members first concentrated on those streams that included their areas of expertise, trying to understand them more fully and generating possible actions. They then took their ideas and proposals to the larger group for discussion. Using the planning chart as a basic guide, the task force developed the details of each intervention activity.

Initial discussion in the task force identified the NAs' acceptance and cooperation in the change process as one of the main implementation problems. An approach to dealing with this issue was the development of more effective work incentives and both formal and informal rewards. Since these would have to provide a means of enhancing the self-esteem of the NAs, the final structural design included upward mobility for them. A two-level job structure was devised with the higher paying level requiring broader skills and increased responsibilities. The two levels not only included more difficult functions, such as anesthesia support and equipment care, but also contained the housekeeping chores previously held by porters. Another important aspect of this structural change was the creation of a new title for the NAs, which more closely described the work that they would be doing. Since NAs not only assisted nurses but directly supported physicians, patients, and other nonprofessional staff as well, their title was changed to operating room assistants (ORAs). The designation ORA I and ORA II corresponded to the two new job levels. These changes were expected to provide the NAs with a clearer identity in the organization, a chance for advancement, and validation of their worth.

Before any of the plans could be implemented, procedures had to be developed for integrating all these new tasks into a working system. After thorough study of all four streams, the staff development and supply coordinators, along with the director, worked out the details of a preliminary work flow design for case turnover and patient transport. Management engineering and the construction coordinator worked on providing temporary quarters for a holding room while the head nurse coordinated efforts to organize a holding room pilot program. When all the procedures were worked out to the satisfaction of the task force and the pilot program for the holding room had been implemented and validated, it was time to include the NAs in further development of the system. A process for sharing the new design with all affected personnel was then developed.

The preliminary work flow design, along with the proposed changes in organizational structure, was presented to all NAs at a group meeting. They were asked to try out the new job design by working in pairs with members of the nursing staff. All agreed to do it. Daily meetings were set up for evaluating and adjusting the system. Because of their extensive knowledge of the NA environment and their eagerness to learn new skills, a smooth running system was created by the new ORAs within two weeks. The daily meetings became a permanent part of the system, providing for feedback, problem solving, and overall departmental communications. These daily meetings served to further the ORAs' identity and feelings of value within the organization.

Simultaneous with this effort was an attempt to gain final approval for a permanent holding room. Since physician support for the concept had been acquired and the goal of providing more service for less had been met, the proposal for modification of office space to contain a permanent holding room was approved by the administration. Once the organizational framework encompassing the center core had been clearly laid out, the needed technical training was provided. This left one final and vital intervention — the selection of a manager for the center core. The task force had expected that the ORAs would perceive this as a positive move but not as much more than that. The reaction was far beyond their expectations. Having a head nurse appointed as their manager brought about the ORAs' final validation as an important and integral part of the OR. Their pride and self-esteem, reinforced through this final action, was demonstrated by their enthusiasm, cooperation, and esprit de corps. The result was that the initial implementation of a critical new system occurred without interruption or compromise of patient care.

8. *Tracking the Change Activities*. Since implementation of the plans yielded a series of activities, some previously planned and some unanticipated, documenting the events provided a way for the organization to see how it was doing and learn from its experiences. The Tracking Stream Chart allowed the director to understand the change process more clearly and, at the same time, manage it more effectively. It showed the progress of the action plan over time, a particularly important function in this instance, because a controlling time factor existed in the Physical Setting stream, the end of construction by July 30.

Developed as the intervention unfolded, the stream diagram resulting from tracking the change activities is shown in Fig. 4–4. The director regularly mapped out each action performed and classified it into its appropriate stream. The task force would then refer to the Stream Tracking Chart to check and analyze progress, comparing it to the original diagnosis and plans and noting the impact of each activity on other activities. This greatly enhanced their ability to proact rather than react, producing a smoother change process. The diagram shown here captures the most salient points so as to provide the essence without getting bogged down in all of the detail.

Tracking across the four streams made it possible to spot

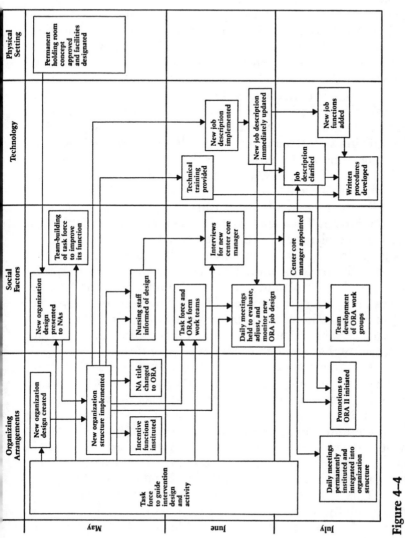

Figure 4-4
Stream Tracking Chart

holes or weaknesses in the change process as it unfolded. For example, a hole is a nonevent, a situation in which an intervention activity should have occurred but did not. Often this is signaled by the occurrence of the missing event some time after it would have been most optimal for it to have occurred. An example of this is shown in Fig. 4–3. The Social Factor activity, "Informing the nursing staff of the new organization design," should have occurred much earlier than it did. It had been omitted from the original plan and was not done until it became painfully obvious that some communication to the nurses was needed. The nursing staff resented not having been told of the change at the same time as the NAs. Since they regarded themselves as higher status than the NAs, they believed that they deserved at least equal treatment.

A comparison of the Stream Planning Chart (Fig. 4–3) and the Stream Tracking Chart (Fig. 4–4) shows that, although many of the planned actions were carried out, not all were actually performed, and some were not performed in the prescribed order or at the anticipated point in time. Certainly, this is as typical of any planning process as it is of any planned change process. But, one of the key benefits of all plans is that they force the implementers to consider the reasons for not taking or for delaying certain actions. It is through this confrontation of plan with reality that wiser choices of action are made.

A further comparison of the two figures reveals that there were several unanticipated actions taken, some even very early on in the process. For example, presentation of the new design to both the NAs and the nursing was not planned. These actions were determined to be necessary for the cooperation and involvement of the two groups. Somehow they were missed in the planning process. However, in the future, one could expect that actions such as these would be anticipated and planned early on.

This is an example of the type of learning that results from carefully tracking the change process and then comparing the actual events to those that were planned. The impact of all this real-time analysis was that the members of the OR learned about the dynamics of their own change process and used their learning to better manage their future efforts at improving the system's functioning.

Summary

This section presented an example of Stream Analysis applied to solving a particularly intractable problem in one organization. It showed how the technique can be used to diagnose the situation, plan actions based on that diagnosis, and finally track the intervention process so that learning about how change takes place in the system can occur. It is noteworthy that the example took place without the help of an outside consultant. Although one would, no doubt, have assisted the process tremendously, the Stream Analysis technique allowed the organization's management to proceed on its own.

The Stream Analysis technique has also been found useful in situations in which a decision has been made about a change and the key task is how to implement it. Some examples might be: designing the new organizational forms needed to operationalize a different organizational thrust, a new technology, changed physical settings, and so on. A description of this type of application is the topic of the next section.

Designing an Organizational Improvement

Stream Analysis, as a diagnostic and planning technique, has clear and obvious application to organizational situations in which things are not going well. But, just as with the general field of OD, Stream Analysis also can be applied to growth-oriented situations. In such situations an organization is functioning well but desires to be more effective and so engages in planned change to improve the way it does things. Here, Stream Analysis is used to help determine what the new organizational situation should look like, what issues need to be addressed to achieve the new organizational form, and what actions are needed in order to get there.

This section presents an example of Stream Analysis used as a tool for understanding all the actions necessary to incorporate a substantial piece of new technology into an organization.[5]

[5]To protect the confidentiality of the organization, any information describing it has been disguised.

This case is not one in which the system was malfunctioning or needed correction. Instead, the organization had been performing well and wanted to enhance its effectiveness by incorporating a new computer-based information system to provide up-to-date data to all members.

The Organizational Situation

Historically, the CJP Company had generated all its reports and schedules by hand, disseminating the information throughout the organization in typewritten form. Although the manual system had worked well up through the 1970s, by the mid-1980s, it became clear that the response time provided by the manual system was too slow to meet new industry demands for rapid competitive pricing decisions. Information from the system concerning productivity levels, market trends, and shifts in customer demands was not readily available. One consequence was that market share was being lost because the organization could not respond in a timely manner without current, up-to-date data.

In July 1985 the manager of one department within CJP decided to explore the possibility of creating a comprehensive computer-based, real-time information system to integrate all the informational and scheduling needs of the department. Early investigation revealed two key facts. First, because of the highly variable character of CJP's products, the new system would need to include a sophisticated and complicated scheduling and tracking capability. And second, since the manual system currently in use required a highly structured organization to support it, it was apparent that the new computer-based system would have significant impact on the department's current organizational structure and the people in it.

At that time, a task force was put together to investigate the situation more deeply and to pick a vendor for all the required computer equipment and associated system design support. The task force first performed a broad assessment of the informational and scheduling needs of the division, and, based on their findings, interviewed several vendors, and selected one who agreed to provide the necessary equipment and service.

1. Formation of a Change Management Team, Collection of Information, and Creation of Stream Diagnostic Chart. Once the vendor had been selected, the task force, now designated as the change management team, turned to the job of detailing what was needed and how to incorporate the new system into the on-going work of the department. The department manager, also a member of the CMT, suggested that Stream Analysis be used to identify systematically all the key issues facing the organization in implementing the change in a planned way.

The task force, in just one hour and a half meeting, first generated a list of concerns, needs, and questions it had about the new system, and then organized the issues into appropriate streams. The Stream Analysis framework focused the group members' thinking and allowed them to move quickly through the process of generating all the relevant data. Extensive discussion of linkages among issues then occurred and, once agreement was reached, the connections were drawn in the chart.

It is important to note that, in this situation, all the pertinent data were gathered in just one session. Very little was added after that. This was possible because of the extreme care that had been taken in the original selection of the CMT membership. Each person in the group carried, in his or her head, a part of all the information needed to implement the new system. Had not all the key actors been part of this group, then more time would have been needed to generate the relevant information.

After the first meeting, the data were transferred, by the department manager, from newsprint to a Stream Analysis form (standard size notebook sheet set up in the stream format). Some refinements in the analysis were made by the department manager at that time, although in general the chart was very complete. The resultant chart (shown in Fig. 4–5) was sent to each team member prior to the second meeting so that adjustments, additions, or questions related to the original analysis could be prepared in advance.

The task force began its second meeting by discussing any new perspectives that had come up on the concerns, needs, and questions they had originally generated; how these three topics were related to one another; which ones could be addressed to-

Figure 4-5
Stream Diagnostic Chart: Questions, Concerns, and Needs

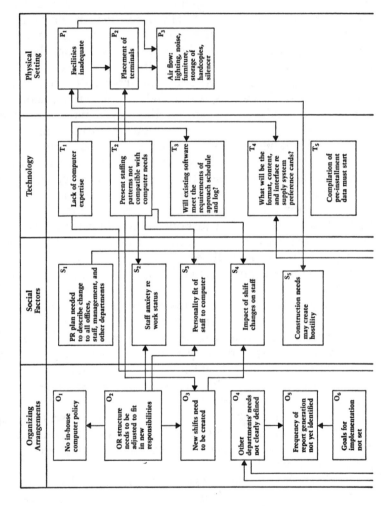

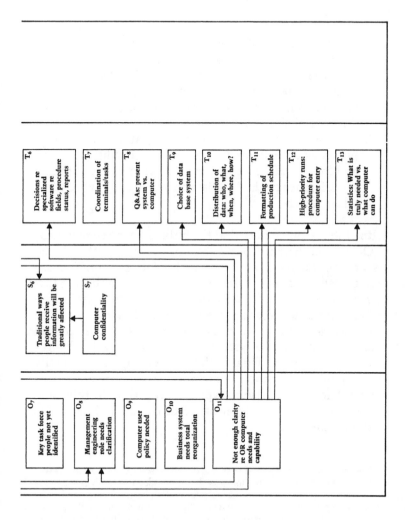

gether as a group; what were the specific potential actions; etc. Because the Stream Diagnostic Chart forms had been sent out in advance, considerable time was saved in this second meeting.[6]

The Stream Diagnostic Chart (Fig. 4–5) shows an array of anticipated issues.

1. Anticipated actions needed ("Organization structure needs to be adjusted to fit in new responsibilities"; "New shifts need to be created"; "PR plans needed")
2. Concerns about the anticipated changes ("Staff anxiety re work status"; "Personality fit of staff to computer"; "Impact of shift changes on staff")
3. Questions that needed answering ("Will existing software meet the requirements vis-à-vis schedule approach and log?"; "What will be the format, content, interface re preference cards?"; "Distribution of data: Who, what, when, where, how?")

It is interesting to note that the bulk of *needs* were located in the Organizing Arrangements stream, *concerns* in the Social Factors stream, and *questions* in the Technology stream. This distribution of issues across streams reasonably reflects the fact that we often tend to see most clearly the structural and administrative policies, procedures, and systems needed to make a change work. At the same time, we worry and are often least certain about how the people in the system will be affected by the changes and how they will react. Finally, the greatest mystery generally revolves around the Technology stream because that is the area in which the least expertise is typically available. In this case, Technology was the area triggering all of the alterations in the rest of the organization.

---

[6]The manager later reported that one of the reasons Stream Analysis was so highly thought of in his organization was that it speeded up the change process considerably while at the same time actually providing better, clearer, and more complete data. In his organization, managers abhor meetings and resent the time it takes them away from their departments. Stream Analysis really impresses them by providing a process that quickly generates data and results. Managers report feeling that much gets accomplished using this technique for planning how to implement a substantial change in the organization.

2. Develop a Stream Planning Chart. The CMT analyzed the Stream Diagnostic Chart and discussed the general actions that would need to be taken to deal with the issue described in each box. Things to watch out for, be concerned about, and integrate with other actions dominated the discussion. Out of all this, the CMT was then able to identify the key areas needing most immediate attention. From this they developed a planning chart (Fig. 4–6) describing the key actions to be taken over the next three months.

Note that this planning chart shows no interconnections among the various change activities. Since great care had been taken identifying the relationships on the diagnostic chart, the CMT did not find it useful to establish those linkages and therefore omitted them. The flow of resultant activities, over time, gave the team the necessary information and they did not feel they needed to note the action interconnections. Instead, the chart was used primarily to pace all change activities over the next three months and assign responsibility for each action to an appropriate manager.

Next to each action item on the planning chart was placed the name of the person or persons responsible for that action. A time frame for completion of the action was also noted and commitments were made by each person to accomplish the activities they were responsible for by the prescribed dates. At each subsequent review meeting, those responsible were asked to report on the progress they had made in completing the tasks to which they had committed. This mechanism turned out to be an excellent way to control and coordinate the activities of the group.

3. Implement Change Activities and Track Change Process. The various plans shown in Fig. 4–6 were implemented over the course of the next three months and the manager of the department tracked the process by noting when an issue on the original diagnostic chart had been resolved. He did this by drawing a diagonal line through each box as it was dealt with. This proved to be a very effective means of communicating progress to the department manager's boss. Discussions of how implementation of the new computer system was going would center around the diagnostic chart and how each of the problems noted there was

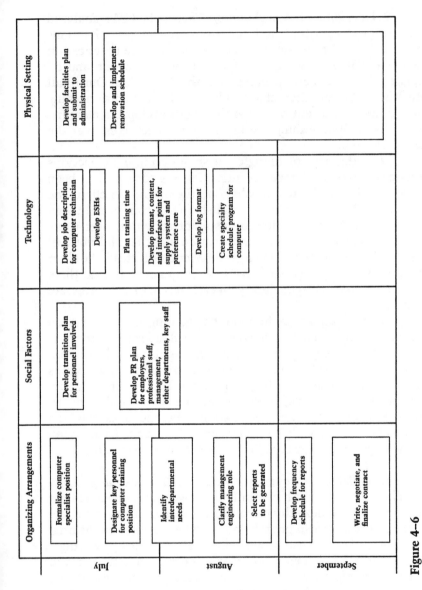

Figure 4-6
Stream Planning Chart: Pre-Implementation

118

being or had been taken care of. In this manner, the department manager could take a "success driven" perspective in reporting progress. The effect was to give the boss a bottom-line, results-oriented report. This is in contrast to the type of "action driven" report that would have evolved if the planning chart had been the basis for communicating progress. In this case, the department manager found the first approach very helpful in understanding the status of the change process.

4. Review Progress and Create New Plans. After the three months covered by the initial plan were up, a review of progress on the project was held and the CMT developed a second three-month plan to guide the implementation of the new system. This new planning chart is shown in Fig. 4–7. As can be noted from the chart, some of the actions planned earlier had still not been accomplished. Most notably, the development of the format, content, and interface for the supply system or preference cards had not been completed. This action was rescheduled and new ones, not previously defined, were also programmed.

The implementation of the new system proceeded more or less as planned and by January of the following year, only seven of the issues defined in the original diagnostic chart had not been resolved. These were clearly identified and work proceeded on them without the need of creating a formal planning document.

Some general observations about this particular project can shed further light on the way the stream approach was used and the impact it had. First, all meetings held as part of this project were kept to a maximum of 90 minutes. CMT members were expected to be prepared for the discussions and a minimum amount of time was wasted during the sessions.

The impetus created by the process of Stream Analysis carried over to the time between meetings with people attending to the activities identified and agreed upon during the previous meeting.

The practice of marking a diagonal line through each box not only provided the manager's boss with a progress report, it also provided the team members with an incentive to complete the activities assigned to them. It was quite embarrassing for individual team members to have all others see on the chart that

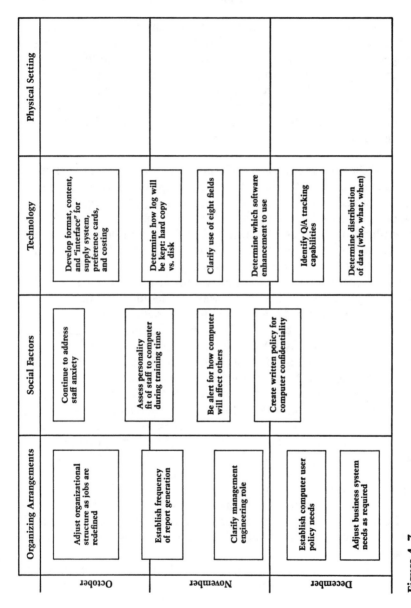

Figure 4–7
Stream Planning Chart: Months 4–6

120

they did not deliver as promised. This was where putting the initials of the responsible team members in each action box paid off.

Finally, after the project had ended, it was clear to all who had participated in it that the detail generated by the Stream Analysis approach was a significant factor in keeping things from falling through the cracks. Very few necessary actions were omitted and, in fact, many which would more than likely have been missed were identified and taken care of in a timely manner.

Summary

This section has described Stream Analysis as a tool for implementing systemic improvements in situations which require the development of new organizational characteristics — that is, new Organizing Arrangements, Social Factors, Technology, and Physical Settings. This redesign of the organization to accommodate new forms of operating can be facilitated by applying Stream Analysis. It assists in identifying all of the streams critical to the effective implementation of any major change and provides a framework for planning and controlling the change process as it unfolds.

Diagnosing a Complex Situation

The third example of the application of Stream Analysis focuses on an organization wanting a broad-scaled diagnosis of its functioning. TRW Components International (TRWCI) had been performing relatively well over the last two years, but its general manager, Doug McCormac, believed that a substantial amount of untapped potential existed in the company and it could be developed only if some of the "nagging problems" which had been plaguing them were identified and resolved. He saw an important opportunity to make the company a more fun and exciting place in which to work as well as one that was even more highly profitable and efficient. Doug learned about Stream Analysis in an executive program on change and thought it would be an excellent way to diagnose his organization's problems and trigger the extensive, long-term improvement process he envisioned.

Background on the Company

TRW Components International was formed to take advantage of the need for highly sophisticated components used by high technology companies world-wide. Their function was to identify suppliers of these items, purchase large lots so as to acquire quantity discounts, inspect and test the components to assure that quality and performance standards were met, and then ship the parts to various manufacturers for assembly into a larger, more complex system. TRWCI had earned an impressive reputation in the industry because it was able to negotiate excellent prices from suppliers, assure high levels of quality, and had an outstanding record for on-time delivery to its customers. As a result, the company generated excellent earnings and had a steep positive growth curve. At the time the change project reported here was launched, TRWCI employed approximately 100 people, the vast majority of whom were located in the company's main facility.

The Change Project

As a prelude to collecting information about the workings and failings of the organization, TRWCI's director Doug Mc-Cormac called his assistant general manager and several of the company's other key executives into his office and discussed his plans to institute a change process based on using the Stream Analysis framework. The executive team agreed to the idea and decided to obtain the help of two outside consultants to assist them in various aspects of the project.

1. Formation of Temporary Change Management Team. Doug first met with the consultants and they, as a group, decided to consider themselves a temporary change management team (CMT). Their plan was to engage in a participative data collection process and to select members for a permanent CMT after observing the involvement of organizational members in that process. They felt that a more effective CMT would result if it consisted of people who really immersed themselves into the diagnostic process and who were not afraid to "speak their minds."

A general plan was established to divide the company up into fifteen- to twenty-person "Productivity-Quality" or PQ teams, to use these teams initially for data collection, and then to use them as a source of ideas for problem solutions and implementation. The PQ teams were each assigned a manager to act as coordinator and to provide a liaison with the top management group.

The change project was to begin with a two-day off-site meeting attended by all the members of the organization. The first morning would consist of the consultants presenting the Stream Organization Model, an overview of Stream Analysis, and a description of the general steps in a planned change process. Employees would be encouraged to ask questions about the information they were receiving so that they could get as clear an understanding as possible about the activities of which they were to be a part. Once the conceptual basis was set, all remaining activity during the off-site meetings could focus on the diagnosis.

2. Information Collection. Prior to the off-site meeting, Doug had written a memo to all employees describing the change process he wanted to initiate and the general thrust of the initial off-site meetings. In it, he asked all employees to think about their jobs and the way the organization functioned, and to make a list of all the problems they saw: the factors keeping them from doing a better job, the things they encountered that reduced the effectiveness of the organization, issues that never seemed to get resolved, and so on. Each person was to bring their problem list to the meetings. There was an assurance from Doug that no punishment or negative consequence would result from any information shared or opinion expressed by employees during this process. Needless to say, some people believed this to be true, but others did not. In any case, every individual walked into the off-site meeting with a list of problems.

The actual data collection activity involved getting all the inputs generated by each of the employees. This was accomplished through the use of the PQ teams. The groups were formed and assigned private areas in which to do their work. Each group was provided a flip chart pad upon which all the problems were to be written. The technique for eliciting information was similar to the one described in Chapter 2. It consisted of going around the table and asking each person, in turn, to present a problem from his or her list. People who did not want to present anything when their turns came would pass.[7] After each person had had the opportunity to contribute a problem, the process was repeated a second, then a third time and continued as long as was necessary. As the list of problems on the flip chart sheets began to grow, new ideas were triggered in the minds of the participants and they began to mention problems that were not originally on their lists. After several rounds, eventually every member of the group passed and the data collection process for that group ended. On average, each group generated from 60 to 120 items.

The next step was for each group to look at the master list it had developed and categorize the problems described on it so as to eliminate overlap and duplication of information. This categorization process was not easy, but it did provide additional benefits above and beyond the information generated. For one thing, as people began to group like problems together, they would expand on what a problem meant to them and how it was similar to another problem on the list. In doing this, each employee began to better understand how others perceived the problems of the organization and whether or not they were the only ones who saw a particular issue as a problem. By discussing difficult issues so openly, it became legitimate to disclose them and inappropriate to hide or deny that things were going badly in the organization. This process began to change system norms on whether or not it was acceptable to discuss problems openly, in the presence of managers or fellow employees who were not close friends.

Once the individual group lists had been "cleaned," they

---

[7]There was one important advantage to this technique of collecting data that is not common to most approaches that do not guarantee anonymity of the respondent: it gives the individual control over when to share "hot" data, if they do so at all. When each person's turn came up, the person could select any item from his or her problem list to share. Early on in the process, only fairly safe issues were expressed. Later on, a few individuals began to propose more delicate problems. At the end, almost everything that was expressed tended to be pretty hot. Some (a few) individuals walked out of the session with items on their problem lists which they did not share. The emphasis was on not pressuring people to disclose information which they found too threatening to reveal in that setting.

were consolidated into one master list consisting of approximately eighty items. Doug reviewed the master list and made a public commitment to continue the problem analysis process and to take appropriate actions as soon as possible. With this, the off-site sessions ended.

3. Formation of Permanent Change Management Team. The permanent CMT, formed within a few days after the end of the off-site meetings, consisted of a cross section of key managers and employees and was selected by Doug, Jerry (his executive director), and the two consultants. Based on the behavior observed during the off-site meeting and Doug and Jerry's prior knowledge, the individuals chosen included people who seemed to be central to the various communication networks operating in the organization and who tended to be outspoken, both for and against the things they saw going on in the company. In addition to not being afraid to say what they thought, the individuals selected had a reputation for being sensible and were well-thought-of by their peers. The new CMT's first responsibility was to do an immediate Stream Analysis of the data. After that, its job was to oversee and monitor all subsequent change actions.

4. Creation of Stream Diagnostic Chart. The CMT met, along with one of the consultants, and began organizing the master problem list into streams and creating the interconnections among the categorized problems. Because of the large number of problems generated by the original process, the consultants did a first pass at their categorization. This draft chart was then presented to the CMT, which discussed each problem, made sure that everyone understood what it meant, and decided whether or not it was properly assigned. Once an agreement was reached as to each problem's classification, interconnections across problems were then identified.

This chart showed all of the problems and interactions agreed to by the CMT members. It was extremely complex and easily decipherable only by the individuals involved in its development. For that reason, the CMT decided not to share publicly this version of the diagnosis but rather to go on and identify the various stories in it and develop separate story charts. It was these story charts that would be disseminated to the rest of the organization and used as a basis for discussion and action.[8]

5. Identification of Core Problems, Themes, and Stories. This part of the diagnostic process was perhaps the most difficult and arduous one. Analyzing the Stream Diagnostic Chart and picking out the key issues became an eye-opening experience for all the CMT members, especially the two top managers who wound up being the topic of one of the key problem stories. The more important stories were identified and rank ordered in terms of how vital they were to the success of the organization. Separate Stream Diagnostic Charts were then made for each of them.

The next step was to obtain feedback from the remaining members of the organization about the preliminary diagnosis generated by the CMT. Each story chart was posted on the walls of the main entrance to the building. Additional blank sheets of paper were also posted on the walls for employees to provide feedback on the diagnoses shown in the charts. Organization members were asked to analyze the materials, judge whether the problems they thought important were being captured by the charts, and if the relationships highlighted made sense and were meaningful. A variety of comments were provided by employees, several of which reflected some underlying hostility not previously captured in the analysis. Additional meetings were held to bring that information to light and incorporate it into the final diagnosis.

The CMT took all the feedback it received and revised the charts as appropriate. The end result was then considered the most complete view of the organization's problems that had ever been generated and it provided the basis for various actions that

---

[8]It should be noted that the charts generated did not contain a Physical Setting stream because none of the problems identified were in this arena. The consultant frequently probed for problems of this type, but organization members consistently believed that no difficulties of the Physical Setting sort existed. It is my belief that they were not clearly seeing the issues in this area but since they could not be convinced of this the consultant reported that he chose not to pursue this point of view any further. Later on, however, the organization expanded into some additional space and discovered that many difficulties existed in what they had been doing that they had not been able to see previously.

followed. The final version of the seven most important story charts are shown in Figs. 4–8 to 4–14.

A key part of the process through which all of these Stream Diagnostic Charts were generated involved the conscious support of differing points of view on what problems meant and how they might be related. Every attempt was made to incorporate the "deviant" perspectives because it was believed that much useful information was contained in these points of view.

There was a second key aspect to the process through which the CMT developed its diagnosis that is worthy of note. Early on in its work, the CMT realized that it often needed more factual data around a problem, data which were not immediately in the heads of the members of the group. So, it created a procedure in which "guest experts" would be invited to the meeting to provide the information needed by the team. For example, if the CMT was trying to understand a problem that had to do with the purchasing function and needed more data on it, the purchasing department manager would be called and he or she would come and attend the meeting and answer questions related to the issue. In this manner, key managers outside of the CMT wound up getting better views of the issues they were confronting because the information they provided to the CMT would generate discussions of which they would be a part. These discussions often brought out new information that the guest did not know anything about or presented new perspectives that helped the guest see old problems in different ways.

The creation of the master Stream Diagnostic Chart, as well as the individual story charts, was a long and rather difficult process for the CMT.[9] It met once or twice per week for approximately two and one-half months with each meeting lasting four to five hours.[10] However, at the end, the group was very confident that it had identified the true problems of the organization and

---

[9]The consultant working with the group served a very useful role in facilitating the process and helping to keep the group on track. Process consultation is a critical function that must be played by someone or else the group interaction can become very ineffective. Edgar Schein's early book, *Process Consultation* (Addison-Wesley, 1969) and his new one, *Process Consultation Volume II* (Addison-Wesley, 1987) provide many useful ideas on this activity.

[10]Total number of meeting hours during this stage was approximately fifty.

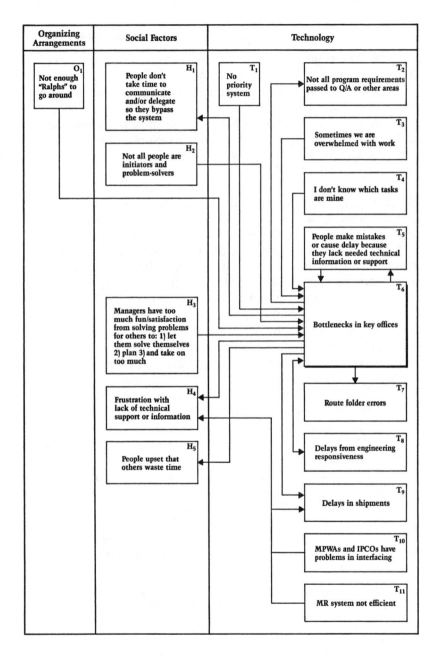

Figure 4-8

Story Chart. Problem 1: Bottlenecks

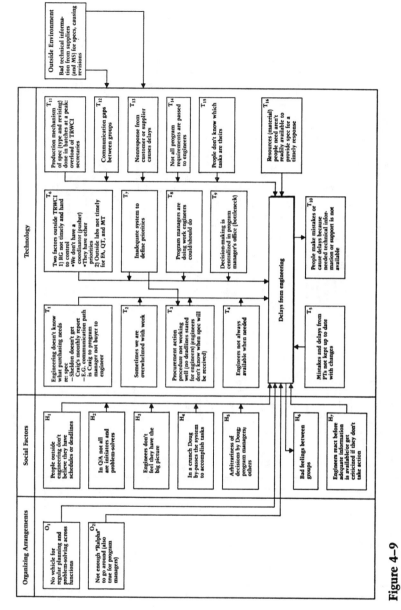

Figure 4–9
Story Chart. Problem 2: Delays from Engineering

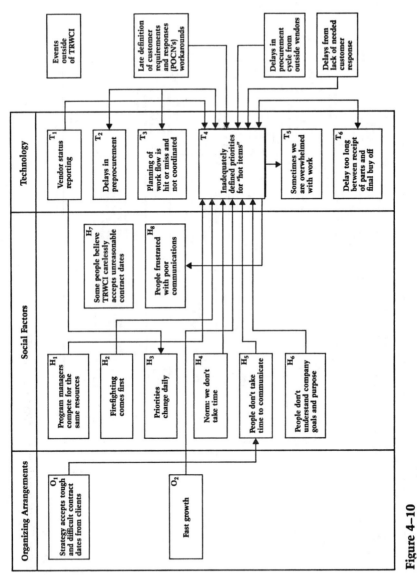

Figure 4–10
Story Chart. Problem 3: Poor Priorities for "Hot Items"

130

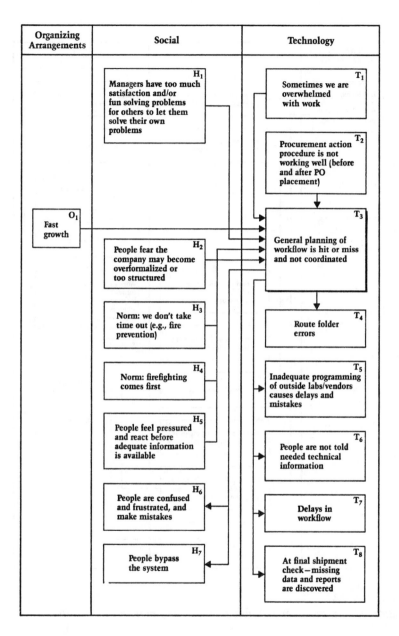

Figure 4–11
Story Chart. Problem 4: Poor Planning of Workflow

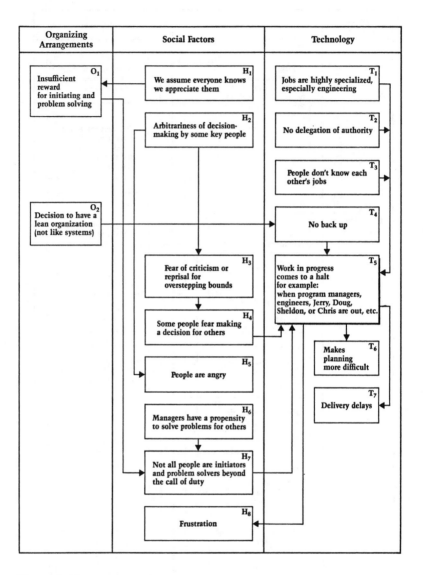

Figure 4–12
Story Chart. Problem 5: Problems When Key Functions Are Out

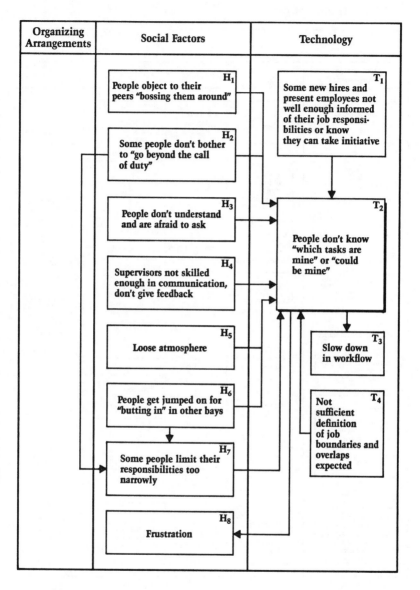

Figure 4–13

Story Chart. Problem 6: People Not Aware of Job Responsibilities (Boundaries)

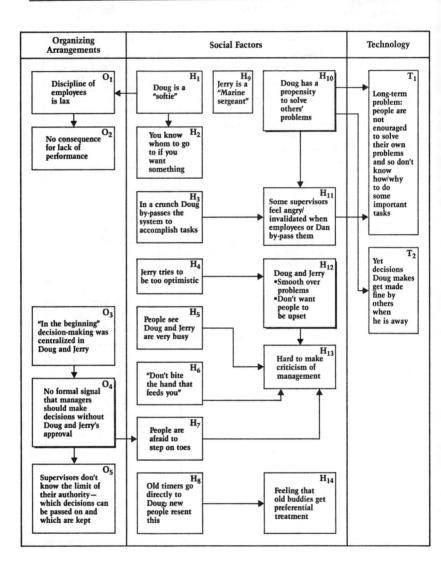

Figure 4–14
Story Chart. Problem 7: Feedback to Doug and Jerry

that it could wholeheartedly support the process of taking action on them.

On reflection, Doug and the other executives, as well as the CMT, believed that the most positive aspect of the process they had gone through was that it had been very participative. Using the charts as a vehicle, a wide range of organizational members had become involved in the process, knew more about the problems they all faced, and felt, as a consequence, more committed to taking the actions necessary to resolve the issues revealed. Most people were now aware of what was going on, tended to agree with the conclusions reached, and felt that their opinions were being heard and valued. All these reactions were quite important for gaining support in implementing the various actions that followed.

One final Stream Chart, called the "superchart," was developed solely by Doug and the two consultants. The eight most important story charts were analyzed and two to three core problems identified in each of them. These core problems were then put together into one chart and their interconnections identified. Doug wanted to put this type of chart together to use as his own personal map of the key issues in the organization. He would not share this chart with other organizational members but would use it as a guide to keeping himself aware of where they were in terms of dealing with this distillation of the most important problems in the system. He also used it as a guide for assessing his own personal behavior change. This superchart is shown in Fig. 4–15.

6. Creating an Action Plan and Implementing Changes.
Although the organization did not formally lay out its actions in a Stream Planning Chart, it did undertake three major sets of activities, all designed to deal with one or more of the major problem stories identified in the diagnosis. First, in the Technology stream, a comprehensive and complex computer system was developed to create a data base for production control. Components could be tracked from the moment they entered the system until they were shipped to the customer. The computer system also was linked to vendors so that rapid communication could occur. Electronic mail and other office automation aids were

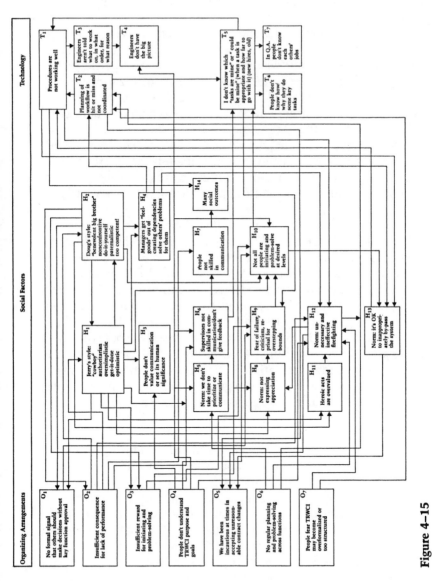

Figure 4-15
Superchart: What Goes Wrong at TRWCI

136

included in the system to speed up communication and co-ordination with the organization. This effort was initiated to deal with key problem areas such as the "bottlenecks" (Problem 1), "delays from engineering" (Problem 2), "poor priorities for 'hot items'" (Problem 3), and so on.

The managerial hierarchy (Organizing Arrangements stream) was also changed to create different assignments for the various managers and departments. Responsibilities were redistributed so as not to continue overloading key individuals as well as to better define what each organizational area was required to do. This action helped deal with issues such as "problems when key functions are out" (Problem 5) and "people not aware of job responsibilities" (Problem 6).

The third major action was to institute a broad-scale training process (Social Factors stream and Technology stream) that would improve both the technical and behavioral skills of organizational members. The program contained technical training (as in principles of electronics), customer training (on who the customers were, how they operated, what their special needs were), and communication training (on interpersonal relationships, group problem solving and decision making, conflict resolution). All members of the organization were exposed to various parts of this training, with special emphasis placed on the communications thrust for managers and supervisors. Overall, this training effort was designed to deal with a wide array of problems that cut across several of the major organizational problem stories.

Summary

This example portrays an extremely complex diagnosis based on Stream Analysis. It demonstrates both the richness and advantages of being able to array the numerous problems in an organization in such a manner that they make sense and can be used as a guide for action. It also shows how Stream Diagnostic Charts can be used to increase communication about the change process as well as to provide a mechanism for promoting the participation of large numbers of members of an organization in the diagnosis itself.

With these three examples in mind, let us now turn to a summary of traps one might fall into when using this technique. The following chapter will list many of the traps I have encountered and a series of tips on how to go about dealing with them.

5

Using Stream Analysis
Tips and Traps

Stream Analysis starts out as a rather simple concept but, in its application, can generate an enormous amount of data and rather complex charts. For this reason, it is important that the user of this approach make every attempt to keep the quantity of information at a manageable level. In this chapter we will discuss many of the key concepts we have learned in using the technique in a variety of organizations.[1] Since a tip often describes a way of avoiding a trap, my discussion will present both together, when appropriate.

Setting the Right Conditions

Prior to launching into a Stream Analysis, several actions can be taken that will tend to increase the likelihood of success in using the technique. First, it is extremely important to set re-

[1]I would like to thank Gary Dexter, Joan Harkness, and Susan Hoffer for their contributions to the development of the ideas presented in this chapter. They all have used Stream Analysis in one or more organizations and were willing to share their experiences.

alistic expectations about the length of time it might take to create a reasonably complex diagnostic chart in a problem situation. Once the data have been collected, a change management team might be expected to need five to six half-day meetings to categorize the problems and identify the key interconnections. Another three to four half-day meetings would then be needed to analyze the chart and identify the core problems and critical stories in the data.

Based on these needs, it becomes critical that a time commitment agreement be reached by all the members of the change management team prior to beginning the process. That agreement can be used as both a guide and a prompt to conclude analysis of the information in a timely fashion.

A second commitment that should be obtained from participants in the diagnostic process revolves around the wording of problems and the impact those words may have on the people responsible for a problem area. Because problems must be worded succinctly in order to fit in a box on a chart, they often take on an exaggerated tone. It is easy for managers to become defensive when they see the problems they have responsibility to solve stated so boldly. So, it is useful to warn managers participating in this process that statements can be exaggerated and that the process precipitates this to some degree. The warning is not intended to dilute the severity of the identified problems so that they become palatable to the people responsible for them. Rather, it is intended to avoid the overreactions that can easily occur when problem-oriented data are placed on charts in this manner. They can appear rather stark and produce a strong impact which might be difficult for many unsuspecting managers to handle.

A further caution exists around the type of people who might be involved in doing an analysis of this type. My experience has shown that individuals who like to conceptualize and use visual representations, who are analytical, and who like to mentally take things apart and put them back together before acting find this approach quite appealing. It is logical, thorough, and step-by-step. In Meyers–Briggs terms, these would be more "sensing/thinking" types of people. At the other extreme, those who like to see the broad gestalt, are more intuitive (the "intuition/feeling" types), and prefer to take action quickly rather than sit back and analyze things get somewhat frustrated with Stream Analysis. They find it too detailed and slow.

It is important not to attempt to use this approach with any group containing a preponderance of this latter type of person. They want to get on with it, to "knock off the analysis and start taking some action," to stop talking about it and make things happen. More than likely, they would not find Stream Analysis very appealing and would not have the patience necessary to complete both the analysis and planning processes.

Mechanics of the Process

Perhaps the area needing the greatest creativity is the process through which the information collected is physically handled and organized into streams. The brief examples already presented make it quite clear that an enormous amount of information can be generated very quickly with this technique. It is important, therefore, to be able to process the data in as efficient a manner as possible. I am presently developing a computer software package that will tremendously improve the process of creating Stream Charts. However, until the time that the programs become available, the data must be manually processed. I would like to present a few hints on how to make that activity more efficient.

Let's begin our discussion at the very basic level of how problems are identified in the first place. In Chapter 2 we suggested that descriptions of problems could be derived through interviews or from questionnaires. Various group interview techniques were proposed that focus on identifying problems. It is about this latter approach that I would like to give some hints.

A common problem when brainstorming issues with a group is that many of the points of view are held by only one person and if these minority perspectives are allowed to remain on the chart, they may create problem overload. One solution is to not place a problem on a final Stream Chart unless at least two people have suggested it and see it as having an impact on the organization's effectiveness.

Once problems have been described, through group brainstorming or some other data-gathering technique, they need to be analyzed for overlaps or duplication, to make sure the same issue is not being described more than once but in different words. An effective way of doing this is to write each problem on a 3 × 5 Post-it® sheet and stick it to a wall so that everyone in the group can see all the problems at once. The group as a whole can then collect common issues together and eliminate any overlap that might exist in the original wordings. In this manner, the data can be reduced, making the next step of problem categorization easier and more productive.

Large flip chart sheets have been used for creating the Stream Charts themselves. If there are numerous problems to categorize, then one stream can be placed on each sheet. Otherwise, it is convenient to place two or all four streams on an individual sheet. The problems can be pasted into their appropriate streams and moved around as the analysis proceeds.

Once the categorization has been completed, it is very helpful to rewrite the problem statements in different colors depending on the stream to which they have been assigned. (Represent each stream with a different color and make all problem statements, boxes, and arrows originating in that stream that color.) The use of color makes it much easier to see the overall flows of arrows and to follow a particular arrow from one box to another.

If the number of arrows grows to the point that the resulting chart becomes too cluttered, a technique I have developed for reducing the complexity might be used. It involves first assigning a code to each problem box. Using the first letter of the first word in the title of each stream along with a number is a simple and straightforward way to code the problem boxes. For example, the first box in the Organizing Arrangements stream would be coded O_1, the second O_2, and so on. The first box in the Social Factors stream would be S_1, the second S_2, and so on. Each box would be assigned a code and interconnections among boxes would be represented by drawing short lines with arrows pointing either into or out of each box. All arrows coming out of a box would do so at the bottom of the box and all arrows going into a box would come in at the top. So, if two boxes were connected, the driving problem would have an arrow coming out of the bottom of its box with the code written next to it of the box to which it was connected. The problem being caused would have an arrow drawn coming into the top of its box. At the base of the arrow would be the code of the problem box from which the arrow came. In this manner, one could quickly identify the origin or destination of any particular arrow. It would also be useful if the arrows were color-coded as suggested above.

Although this technique does much to reduce the clutter of a Stream Chart, it has some disadvantages. It makes it a bit more difficult to get the overall gestalt of the interconnections by stepping back and seeing the entire chart and getting a "feel" for the aggregated flows. By both using color and having all interconnecting lines drawn completely, a broad impression of the general direction of causal relationships is much more easily acquired. It is interesting to note that this broader gestalt is typically born out by more quantified analyses such as frequency counts of the paired relationships. So being able to get a broad perspective by seeing the chart in its entirety is not a trivial price to pay for the sake of creating an uncluttered chart. In this tradeoff the user of this approach must decide which technique is best based on the particular characteristics of the analysis being done.

One final suggestion on the issue of messiness and complexity in the Stream Charts: I have found that, during the period in which they are being developed, it is extremely useful to redraw the charts at the end of each problem identification session. Since a complete chart is typically not created in one meeting, much confusion can be avoided if all of the lines drawn on them can be redone to create a neat and tidy chart. At the following meeting, participants appreciate much more fully both the progress in their work as well as the broader patterns that are developing.

Creating Stream Diagnostic Charts

Charting problems can be facilitated by making sure that the issues identified are, in fact, problems, rather than solutions disguised as problems. For example, often a situation in which costs are out of control may be stated as "Need a system to control costs." This way of presenting the problem is simply a solution — a cost control system — disguised as a problem statement. Put in this manner, the normal action would be to create a new cost control system. Other alternatives, some of which may be more appropriate to the situation, exist, but are essentially blocked out because of the way the problem has been stated. If, on the other hand, the problem was described as "Costs are out of control," then this would open up a new set of possible actions, only one of which is to create a cost control system. It is safe to say that the great preponderance of inappropriately stated problems are of this form. Organization members are so action oriented that they often see problems in the form of pre-conceived solutions and are not aware of the limitations this places on their abilities to generate the best solution for any given situation.

Stream Analysis is designed to create a comprehensive mosaic of the problems within an organization. In doing so, it guides organization members to discover more fundamental, or core, problems in the organization's functioning. As originally described, however, the process only helps by pointing to previously identified problems as core problems. Suppose other core problems exist that have not been specifically revealed by one of the data gathering techniques. How can we know that the problems we think are core, in fact, actually are?

To achieve this deeper understanding, for every core problem identified, conduct an additional analysis to ensure that the most fundamental level has been tapped. This added work consists, very simply, of probing each core problem for its causes and roots. "What is driving this problem? What causes this problem to happen?" are both questions that could be asked of every core problem identified through the normal Stream Analysis process. By doing this, the change management team, as a group, can unveil deeper issues, the ones most significant for concerted action. Pushing past the point at which the normal process ends can add substantially to the validity of the analytical approach.

A third suggestion that can improve the creation of the Stream Diagnostic Chart is related to the process of classifying problems into streams. Often the change management team can get bogged down in deciding whether a problem belongs in one stream or another and lose sight of the fact that shared understanding of the problem is the main goal, not "correct" assignment of any one problem. Although it is important to be as logical and consistent as possible in stream assignment of problems, that is not the fundamental purpose of the process. Rather, it is to provide a structure around which key organization members can all discuss a problem until they agree on exactly what it looks like. Often solutions are misguided or not strongly supported because all the parties involved did not see the problem in the same way and therefore could not see common solutions. The Stream Analysis process makes it possible for shared understanding of problems to evolve as organizational members struggle with which stream to assign a problem to. In this struggle they uncover the full dimensions of a problem, the perspectives held by each member of the CMT. Once the shared understanding has been achieved, specific assignment of the problem to a stream becomes less important. There should be face validity to the assignment, but it is not required that the exactly perfect assignment be made. For some problems this is an impossibility anyway.

My next set of suggestions relates to the process of creating the interconnections among problems. As noted above, one of the difficulties in implementing this approach to diagnosing a system is that so many interconnections get identified that the resulting Stream Chart is somewhat unreadable. One approach to limiting the number of interconnections is to ask each member of the CMT to pick out the interconnection they see as the most important one and to place it on the chart. Once this has been done, the chart is analyzed and explanations are given by each person describing their reasoning. The process is repeated four or five times, depending on the number of people participating in the process, until patterns begin to emerge. At this point, it is often appropriate to review the entire chart and begin to remove interconnections that, in light of all the discussion and new awareness that has been generated, do not appear as important as they did originally. Through this process, it is possible to expand or contract the number of interconnections and achieve the degree of complexity that can be handled by the team doing the analysis.

One final note on arrow drawing: For some of the interrelationships, the CMT will find it difficult to decide which way the interconnecting arrow should be pointed. The normal inclination will be to have it pointing in both directions. Avoid doing this. Force a decision on direction. When it comes right down to it, people will be leaning, ever so slightly, in one direction or the other. Find that direction and draw the arrow accordingly. The purposes of pushing for a decision, one way or the other, are twofold. First, it trains the CMT to not take the easy way out when a direction is not obvious. Usually, after discussion and analysis, the direction becomes clear to the group members. If the group doesn't push itself to that point, it will never achieve it. Sometimes getting to the point of clarity requires lots of hard work and, unless trained to do so, the CMT will not be inclined to work that hard. A second reason for requiring that the arrows point only in one direction is simply that the resulting analysis is made easier if there are no two-headed arrows. Stories will be more obvious if the flow of a problem can be tracked. Two-headed arrows potentially block those flows and make it more difficult to pick out the patterns of problems and recognize a problem loop.

Diagnosis should not be accomplished at one sitting. It helps to let the ideas and analyses percolate a bit before returning to them. Therefore, it is reasonable to do one or two rounds of the specification of arrows, then adjourn the meeting. This makes it possible to redraw the charts between meetings, a key part of the process, because at each redrawing it is important to place those problems that have many arrows drawn into them at or near the bottom of the chart, and to place those problems that have many arrows coming out of them at or near the top of the chart. The result is that the arrows will tend to flow downward, from the core problems to the symptomatic problems. This type of flow will make later analysis simpler in that the two types of problems will be easier to spot, visually. More important, however, it will make it easier to see the strings of interconnected problems that make up the stories of organizational ills. It is through the stories that the diagnostic richness of this approach is most clearly demonstrated.

Analyzing Problem Charts

The most important suggestion I can give about this phase in the process is to reiterate the last point made in the preceding section. The general analysis should not begin until the charts are redrawn so that the arrows flow downward and the core problems tend to be at the top of the chart while the symptoms are at the bottom. This makes discussion of these two types of problems simpler, and it also allows for easy addition of the more fundamental core problems that begin to surface as probing of the causes of the core problems proceeds (see discussion above). Having all of the more basic problems at the top of the chart also makes it easier to pick up any theme that might exist among the core problems. These themes could be overlaid on a subset of core problems distributed more or less horizontally across the top of the chart. For example, a subset of core problems might indicate that managers are not attending to their management tasks but instead are more involved in the technical decisions that drive the company or in the administrative details of implementation. Taken together, this group of problems presents a broader, more pervasive, and potentially more important macro problem than any of the individual core problems. The importance of this becomes clear when we begin to consider what the necessary actions might be to deal with the overriding theme. Very clearly, the actions taken would look somewhat different than the collection of actions one might develop to resolve each problem of that set separately.

Problem clusters, which are problems linked vertically down the chart, make up stories about the organization. They are made easier to identify when all causal relationships are drawn to flow in the same direction — downward. This makes them easier to spot and weave together into a more cohesive whole. It is this interconnected set of problems that creates the problem story that also will tend to require a somewhat different set of actions to attack as a whole than the actions that would be needed to deal with each problem in the set separately.

Stories, as well as core problem themes, can be isolated from the basic Stream Diagnostic Chart and put on separate charts. This makes it possible to see the clusters more clearly and to appreciate how the problems shown are interrelated. Often, an all-encompassing label can be attached to a theme or story which can then be used as shorthand for communicating about it in the organization. In one of the examples described earlier, the story label identified was "Firefighting Mentality." This label was used to describe a series of interconnected problems that, when put together, created this mode of organizational functioning. Problems such as "Always behind schedule," "People not rewarded for getting things done early," and "Information not received in a timely fashion," were some of the components of the ad hoc, crisis-oriented, firefighting mentality.

In this same project, a cartoon of a firetruck was used to represent this mentality and became a clear symbol which communicated the set of subproblems related to this issue. Although it did not occur in this project, organizational members could have used the symbol of the firetruck as a way of giving each other feedback whenever they saw firefighting behavior in action. People could have said things to each other like, "Here goes the firetruck again," or "Let's get the firetruck out for this one." They also might have placed little firetruck stickers on memoranda that reflected the firefighting mentality that the group was trying to overcome. All of these symbolic means of communication could have been part of an intervention developed to deal with this set of problems.

We have found, in our work with a variety of organizations, that the "storytelling" approach is a potent way of both analyzing the data in the charts and communicating to others what the main problems in the organization are. If one is able to weave a story together, it does much to verify the validity of the interconnections and to raise the consciousness of the organization members that problems exist in complex structures rather than in simple isolation. Storytelling also becomes an invaluable aid in training the members of the CMT in effective ways to communicate their findings to outsiders. In one organization, the CMT was charged by the board of directors of the organization to find out what was going wrong and to report back. Each member, during analysis of the Stream Charts, learned how to use the data to tell stories about the problems of the organization. In the reporting process, various members of the CMT (some from the lowest levels of the organization) told stories about the key problems and had a profound impact on the board with this process. The board members remarked that they felt they really understood what was going wrong because of the combination of the charts and the ability of the CMT members to weave the problems together into stories.

One note of caution: In the development of stories, attempt to limit the number of core problems that are part of any one story. Three to four core problems per story seem to be the maximum number to include. If too many core problems are part of any particular story, the effect of the story is diluted and it becomes too broad and all-encompassing. In effect, all of the Stream Chart represents one massive and complex problem story. Taken all at once, it is impossible to understand, much less plan appropriate action to resolve the issues. On a simpler level, the same is true for stories that include too many core problems. They are too complex to understand and effectively resolve.

A common trap that befalls almost everyone when working with the Stream Charts is that people begin to suggest solutions before the problems are fully understood. It is very important for users to continue to keep the focus of discussion during the diagnostic stage on the problems, not solutions. A point made earlier should be repeated here. Often problems are stated in the form of solutions. When this occurs, it does not allow for a truly rich understanding of exactly what is going on. Instead, the problem is narrowly understood only in the context of the solution presented. In the example given earlier that confused a solution (a cost control system) with a problem, an understanding of the situation is framed in the context of a control system. Solutions then revolve around what kind of control system should be developed, what its characteristics should be, and so forth. If the problem is framed as one in which costs are out of control, then the solutions that are possible expand and now one can talk about what is causing the costs to be as they are, what alternatives exist that could counteract some of the forces causing the costs to be out of control, and so on. This more complete understanding of the problem and all potential solutions is made more possible when problems are stated as problems rather than as solutions.

Two other phenomena frequently occur in the problem analysis phase that are worth mentioning. First, often groups can get stuck in identifying the key focus of a story and are not open to alternative perspectives. They seem to have all the components, including what they believe to be the appropriate focus, but can't seem to put together a unifying story. They struggle and struggle and finally discover that a completely different focus exists. Once this new perspective is identified, the entire story hangs together very well. Had they been more open to a different focus at the very beginning, the time invested could have been used more efficiently. An example of this occurred in one group that had been developing a story around a set of problems whose main focus was the negative effects of not having enough people to accomplish all of the necessary tasks. After an hour of trying to put the collection of interconnected problems into this story line, someone suggested that maybe the true focus of the story was not the shortage of personnel, but rather the mix of skills that they had in the existing people in the system. Once this new focus was proposed, it was clear that it fit and served to unify the collection of problems quite adequately.

A second process often occurring during problem analysis is that the group gets stuck in identifying and agreeing on exactly what a particular problem is. It turns out that this difficulty is a clue that the problem is really a higher order problem and that is the reason the group can't pin it down. For example, one group was discussing how information about problems gets suppressed in the organization. Some blamed the manager and said that he chewed people out when they brought him bad news. Others said that everyone in the organization was overly critical, making it difficult for a person to talk about things that weren't going right and seeking help. The group tried to pin down exactly what the problem was but they could not. Finally, the consultant working with the group suggested that maybe the real problem was in the culture of the organization and in the norms against risk taking. When this was suggested, all the members of the group agreed and were able to provide a piece of the problem from their own perspectives. Up to that point, all the pieces had not fit together because the problem was being conceived at too low a level of abstraction.

Creating Stream Planning Charts

Probably the most important point in the preparation of the Stream Planning Charts is to insist that almost every action placed on the chart relate to something identified in the Stream Diagnostic Chart. Often, people in organizations, especially managers, have pet solutions that they like to apply to problems whether or not they fit those problems well. One would be surprised how often they creep into action plans without really matching up with any clearly identified problem, theme, or story. For the sake of both efficiency and effectiveness, it is important to keep extraneous actions out of the change plan. One way to structure this goal into the planning chart itself is to create some space in a corner of each action box and place in it the code for the problem(s) it is designed to affect. If the action is intended to deal with a story or theme, then assign a code to each story or theme and enter that code in the appropriate spot in the action box. This simple technique will force the CMT to assess each action in light of the problems it is designed to resolve. It will also help outsiders to understand why a particular action is being taken. This could lead to more commitment on the part of organization members outside the CMT to the actions planned. If they have a clear idea as to why something is being done, they are more likely to support it than if they don't.

A second, more "mechanics of the process" type of hint is to draw the planning charts in the same four colors as the problem charts. Maintaining a similar color code makes it easier for people to go back and forth from one chart to the other and match how the plans relate to the problems. This supports the suggestion above of coding the actions with the problems they aim to resolve. Adding the colors to the process further facilitates the process of matching actions to problems.

Communication Role of Charts

Much of the resistance that occurs in any planned change process can be traced to the ambiguity inherent in the situation. People do not know what is going on and how it will affect them and the things they think important in the organization. One reaction to this lack of information is to hold on to the old way of doing things and resist the changes being proposed. The Stream Analysis format provides a useful method for improving the flow of information about the things that are going to happen, why they are planned, and once the change process is in motion, what is going on. The planning chart conveys what is going to happen, the problem chart establishes why those actions are being taken, and the tracking chart describes what has gone on.

In order for these charts to be useful communication devices, they must be placed in public places in the organization. One organization placed their problem charts in the main entryway of their building. Every day when each person walked into work he or she would pass right by them. When the Stream Diagnostic Chart was initially posted, additional sheets of paper were taped up beside it. The purpose of the additional paper was to obtain reactions from all the employees who had not been directly involved with the analysis. They had provided the initial data but had not been part of the process since that point. The blank sheets (or graffiti space, as it was called by the CMT) were there for anyone who wanted to comment on the analysis. Suggested questions for the employees to ask themselves about the analysis were: Are the problems you see as key included in the chart somewhere? Is there anything important that hasn't been included in the chart? Does the overall chart make sense to you as representing all the problems in the organization? Employees could respond to these questions on the graffiti sheet or make any comments they wished. After several days the graffiti sheets were taken down and analyzed and the information incorporated into the charts wherever appropriate. The revised charts were then posted so that people could see that their inputs were dealt with in some manner. If a piece of information was not included in the chart, an explanation for the reason behind its omission was given.

Another way to get people more involved is to display the charts in some public manner and ask employees to put their name next to any problem they would like to work on. This gives people an opportunity to help resolve the issues they think most important to the organization. This approach works best with smaller organizations and with supervisory or management personnel who have more discretionary use of their time rather than with first level people who are more tightly tied to machinery or the tasks they must perform.

Disseminating information about the change process can

also be accomplished by reducing the charts to 7 × 11-inch sheets and giving them out to relevant organization members. The way they are presented gives out signals about whether or not they are important documents and how they should be treated. If the charts are placed in accetate sheets and enclosed in binders, they take on a more important form and are treated differently by organization members. When everyone has a set of the original charts, they can use them periodically as a source of discussion in meetings reviewing the progress of the change activity. Having charts available, especially the Stream Diagnostic Charts, makes it easier to point out progress made in solving problems. One can refer to the chart and see how much has been done. More public posting of the problem charts to the organization at large can also accomplish the same purpose if it is preceded by announcements highlighting both the progress made and the distance still left to go.

General

It is important to recognize the flexibility inherent in the graphics side of the approach. I have established four streams of problems, plans, and actions as the basis for the technique. I did so because each stream is tied into the framework used to conceptualize the organization. If someone else has another framework that specifies a different set of variables, then the ones I propose can be replaced by others that seem to be more appropriate to the user. If someone likes the four I use but wants to add others, then the technique is flexible enough so the number of streams can be expanded and the same principles for analysis and planning applied. The result will be more complex because of the added streams, but nevertheless still useful. If one of the streams proposed is not seen as changeable and the user does not believe that it adds anything to the analysis, then it can be omitted. One organization deleted the Physical Setting stream for this reason and conducted a very thorough analysis. The basic point is that the approach is reasonably flexible. It provides a structure around which to organize your own views of the organization. The framework contributes to understanding by helping users to systematize their thinking about organizational problems and the actions they wish to take to solve them.

Users of Stream Analysis have reported that going through the process has an important effect on the level of development of the group. The abilities to resolve differences, solve problems, make decisions, communicate more effectively, understand another's point of view are all enhanced as one consequence of the process. As a team works on developing the analysis, all of the dynamics that can inhibit effective team functioning are brought to the surface. Teams learn how to work together more effectively as they resolve the various issues they face in performing the analysis. The end result is that they grow as a problem-solving and decision-making team. This effect should not be ignored by proponents of the Stream Analysis method. It is a very valuable side benefit to the use of the technique.

A final bit of advice: Don't collect too much data. The technique promotes the generation of data. It is possible to drown in the amount of data collected. Be sure to take care to reduce the quantity of information by making decisions about what seems to be important and what is not. Eliminating the seemingly less important runs the risk of actually throwing out something of value. This could happen, but the process is so self-correcting in that questions are always being asked about what is causing something or another that, if something important is discarded, it will tend to reappear at a later date. The simple prescription is to limit the data generated to the amount that your organization can handle.

Conclusions

The Stream Analysis approach is designed to help both managers and practitioners of change to more effectively diagnose complex systems, to plan change interventions guided by that diagnosis, and to track intervention activity as a means of better managing the overall process of change. The tips for using Stream Analysis described here are but a few of the many possible ways to improve the application of this approach. The reader will discover many more in the process of using the Stream Analysis framework. My most important suggestion for the user is to search continually for modifications that will most closely adapt Stream Analysis to the particular organizational situation in which it is applied. The method is sufficiently robust to accept alterations and will be more effective when "customized" for each specific change effort.

6

Summary

The main purpose of this book was to present Stream Analysis, a graphics-based technique for diagnosing an organization's problems, planning the actions or interventions needed to deal with those problems, and tracking exactly what was done so that the organization can learn how to change itself most effectively. Since I believe that the best use of any change technique occurs when the individuals leading the change process understand the conceptual underpinnings of the approach they are using, I described an organizational perspective extensively. Called the Stream Organization Model, this approach views individual behavior as the key mediator between the basic characteristics of an organization and its outcomes. A logical consequence of this view is that meaningful long-term organizational change occurs only when the organization's members change their behaviors and sustain those changes over an extended period of time. The key to successful organizational change, therefore, is to figure out what it will take to get people in the organization to change their behavior. For help on this matter I turned to two prominent theories in organizational sociology and individual psychology — systems theory and social cognitive theory.

From systems theory, I drew the perspectives that most

organizations in today's world exist in turbulent environments to which they must respond; that they are formed to achieve some purpose(s); that they consist of a variety of subsystems or parts, each designed (ideally) with the purpose(s) in mind; that all these parts are interconnected in some way or another with the intention of facilitating achievement of the organization's purpose(s); that organizations create outputs that generate resources needed for continued viability; and finally, that organizations constitute the environment in which each individual employee works. This last point then drove me to develop a perspective on why individuals in an organization behave as they do and what might be done to change their behaviors on the job.

The view presented of why people behave the way they do in organizations is based on social cognitive theory which emphasizes the importance of the work environment people are in and how they might use signals from it to make choices about job-related behaviors. It proposes that behavior change is precipitated by systematically altering the work setting so that the messages people receive about the most appropriate job-related behaviors are also changed. For maximum effectiveness in precipitating behavior change, these messages must all point to the same, new, more organizationally desirable behavior.

People behave the way they do in organizations because the job environment in which they work affects their sense of efficacy (their beliefs about their own abilities to perform particular behaviors on the job), their outcome expectations (their views about the likelihood that their own behavior will lead to particular outcomes) and finally, the value they place on the various outcomes which might result as a consequence of having performed the behaviors signaled by the work setting. The key issue for understanding why people do what they do is in conceptualizing the work setting, that is, determining the important dimensions of the social and physical environment in which people work.

The model described proposes that the work setting consists of four main dimensions, or streams — Organizing Arrangements, Social Factors, Technology, and Physical Setting — each made up of a series of components. From these components come the messages about on-the-job behaviors, messages that affect the individual employee's efficacy expectations, outcome expectations, and valences. Since work settings are complex, each organizational member is bombarded with a wide variety of signals. If, in general, the signals contradict each other and point to different behaviors, then the behavioral responses of organizational members will also be contradictory and more than likely result in mixed, uncoordinated actions on the part of the employees as a group. On the other hand, if the signals are somewhat more consistent, one could expect more coordinated, directed behavior, even though there will still be variations in behavior based on the fact that all individuals are different and will process the messages they receive somewhat differently.

Behavioral change results when the job environment is altered. A change in any of the four organizational dimensions will begin to send new signals about behavior to each organization member. If the change is a significant one, the signals will be quite strong. If it is less substantial, the signals will be weaker. In any case, the signals from one changed dimension may be reinforced or contradicted by the signals coming from the remaining work setting dimensions. If the change is reinforced one would expect to see some behavioral change consistent with the work setting change. If the change is contradicted, one cannot easily predict what would happen. Some individuals would change in the expected manner while others would not. The pattern of response would be heavily determined by exactly how the change in one organizational dimension interacts with the existing designs of the remaining three. Establishing and maintaining consistency across the four organizational streams is the key to coordinated and effective functioning of the organization. How is this accomplished? What mechanism might exist which would serve this function?

The main factor that helps to establish and maintain consistency in the design of the four work setting streams is the organization's purpose. Purpose plays an important role in focusing the organization. It specifies the reason(s) for organizational existence and, as such, provides a basis for determining whether or not any particular decision is in the best interests of the organization. Before any decision is made, decision makers can ask themselves whether or not the decision contributes to the achievement of the organization's purpose(s). Purpose plays a second important role by helping to interpret, for the organization, the environment in which it operates; that is, it provides a set of lenses for viewing the environment and attaching meaning to the things that are seen there. Out of this meaning can come a set of decisions about what actions the organization might take to respond most appropriately to environmental conditions (actions such as product choice and mix, advertising strategy, pricing strategy, and so on). Of more relevance here are actions that focus on how the work setting dimensions should be designed in order to achieve the organization's purpose in the particular environment that was just observed. In this sense, the organization's purpose is the interface between the four main streams of the organization and the environment in which the organization operates.

Similarly, the individual is at the interface between the dimensions of the organization and the outcomes that it generates. If one wishes to improve the outcomes produced by the organization, then behavior must be changed. If one wants to change the behaviors of individuals in the organization, then the characteristics of the work setting must be changed. In order to most effectively change the characteristics of the work setting in a way such that the resulting signals sent to the individual employee are consistent, a method for understanding what is going wrong and for planning corrective action could be quite useful. Stream Analysis is such a method. It is based on the assumptions that the four work setting dimensions are the key factors in determining on-the-job behavior, that the four dimensions are interconnected, and that identifying what must be changed can be facilitated by seeing organizational malfunctionings as driven by patterns of problems rather than by isolated issues.

More specifically, Stream Analysis graphically represents the four dimensions of the work setting and provides a framework for managing a planned change process. The first stage of intervention, diagnosing the organization's problems, can be accomplished by placing all identified problems on a Stream Diagnostic Chart, organized to reflect the four key dimensions. The Stream Organization Model specifies that the four organizational dimensions, now called *streams*, are all interconnected. Therefore, problems identified in each of the streams would also be interconnected.

Drawing the more important problem interconnections on the chart helps uncover the organization's core problems, separating them from symptoms. Problems that are symptoms often receive the most "press." People discuss them, complain about them, and in general, everyone is quite aware of them and often believes that if they were resolved, everything would be just great. In fact, however, it is the core problems that are most important, for they drive intermediate problems that then drive the symptoms. Sifting through the morass of problems typical to most organizations and separating core from other problems is not an easy task. Usually it is quite a confusing process unless aided by some systematic approach that highlights the differences in importance and centrality of problems. Stream Analysis accomplishes this by graphically representing problems in such a way that core problems are highlighted in one way and symptoms in another.

Stream Analysis further assists in understanding the organization's difficulties by highlighting problem themes and problem stories. Problem themes describe sets of core problems, all with a common thread through them. They might provide different pieces of a larger problem or might be different manifestations of more complex issues. Problem stories, on the other hand, are a group of problems through which a sequential linkage exists. So a core problem leads to an intermediate problem, which leads to another intermediate problem, and so on until the chain ends, usually at a symptom. In either case, being able to see problems in complex patterns makes it possible to plan more effective action.

Once a diagnosis has been completed, the Stream Analysis chart format, in a slightly modified form, can be used to plan the needed changes. Each action planned should map into one of the problems or problem themes or stories specified in the diagnostic process. In planning changes, care must be taken to assure that each intervention not only deals with the problems identified but also alters the four organizational dimensions in such a way that the new messages they deliver to organizational members are consistent in that they all point toward the same new behaviors. The changes must affect the individuals' efficacy and outcome expectations as well as their outcome valences in such a manner that they will alter their behaviors in the desired direction.

The final phase of a Stream Analysis approach involves tracking the intervention process as it unfolds. The tracking of change activity not only provides information about the events that actually occur as compared to the ones that were planned, but it can also provide a historical record of what went on so that the organization can learn about its own change processes. This latter function makes improvement in future change activity possible because the change leaders will be able to more intelligently decide on what actions to take based on what they learned out of the effects of actions taken in the previous change activity.

Stream Analysis can be used in a variety of change situations. Three specific ones were highlighted here. First was an organization suffering from a clearly circumscribed problem which needed to be diagnosed and a systematic change process planned. Stream Analysis was used to identify the core issues in the situation and create a change plan to deal with them. Second was an organization in which the major change to be accomplished was already known. In this case, Stream Analysis was used to identify all the dimensions important in designing and implementing the change. Finally there was an organization requiring a broad-based diagnosis to identify the more specific issues impeding effective performance.

Briefly, application of the Stream approach in these three cases usually (but not always) involved the following steps:

1. Create a change management team (CMT).
2. Collect information on issues in the organization.
3. Categorize issues and place them on a Stream Diagnostic Chart.
4. Draw interconnections among issues on the Stream Diagnostic Chart.
5. Analyze the chart and identify core problems, stories, and themes.
6. Create a Stream Planning Chart to guide actions prescribed by the diagnosis.

7. Implement the plan.
8. Document intervention activity on a Stream Tracking Chart.

Stream analysis, as a change management tool, can help managers and consultants more effectively lead planned change processes. It can be used by managers alone or with the aid of consultants. Certainly, the more skilled the resources applied to any change situation, the more likely successful change will evolve. From this perspective, involvement of a skilled consultant in the use of Stream Analysis would add immensely to the potential success of any change project. However, it is important to emphasize that a key aspect of the Stream Analysis approach is that it helps managers independently guide their own change processes and gives them increased control over when they need to call in specialized resources to help them accomplish a specific change. Instead of being dependent on any outsider, change leaders can now call in the outsiders when they are needed. This gives the managers more ownership over leadership of the process and should, as a consequence, result in more commitment on their part to make the change process work.

In conclusion, the Stream Analysis technique was developed as a tool to improve planned change activity. It is rooted in a perspective that describes organizations as changeable systems and individuals as the key element in any effort to alter system functioning. Users of this technique should be helped in their efforts to enhance organizational performance and employee development. Overall, I see the main advantages to using Stream Analysis as the following:

1. The process of assigning problems to streams and making interconnections really drives toward understanding the core issues at work in the situation and creating a shared understanding about them. Shared understanding of the organizational situation is fundamental for creating an effective change process.
2. Joint planning of actions and the creation of an action chart leads to greater commitment to those interventions generated.
3. Use of charts as a communication tool for those not di-

rectly involved in the diagnostic and planning process reduces resistance and cynicism about the change process and enhances involvement and commitment to it.

4. The approach is relatively simple, yet flexible and can be made as complex as necessary. The number or title of columns can be increased, decreased, or changed to make it more relevant to how a user sees the major organizational variables. It also can be either microscopic or macroscopic, creating any level of detail desired.

5. Finally, Stream Analysis brings a systemic and systematic perspective into the process of planned organizational change.

The challenges facing anyone trying to change an organization are many, yet comprehensive approaches for helping to achieve change are few. Stream Analysis is a technique that appears to be a contribution in that regard. In the end, however, the quality of any change effort primarily rests on the capabilities of the individuals involved with it. Stream Analysis is only a tool for enhancing those capabilities.